THE POLITICAL TRANSFORMATION OF SPAIN AFTER FRANCO

THE POLITICAL TRANSFORMATION OF SPAIN AFTER FRANCO

JOHN F. COVERDALE

PRAEGER PUBLISHERS
Praeger Special Studies

New York • London • Sydney • Toronto

Library of Congress Cataloging in Publication Data

Coverdale, John F   1940-
    The political transformation of Spain after
Franco.

    Includes index.
    1.   Spain--Politics and government--1975-
2.   Spain--Economic conditions--1975-   I.   Title.
JN8209 1979.C68   320.9'46'083   78-19777
ISBN 0-03-044326-1

PRAEGER PUBLISHERS
PRAEGER SPECIAL STUDIES
383 Madison Avenue, New York, N.Y. 10017, U.S.A.

Published in the United States of America in 1979
by Praeger Publishers,
A Division of Holt, Rinehart and Winston / CBS, Inc.

9   038   987654321

———————◆◇◆———————

To the memory of my father,
Philip J. Coverdale, Jr.,
and of my brother,
Philip J. Coverdale, M.D.

———————◆◇◆———————

PREFACE

Even a cursory comparison of the Spanish Constitution of 1978 with the fundamental laws by which Spain was governed under Franco reveals the extraordinary political changes the country has undergone in recent years, although their scope cannot be fully appreciated unless one has lived there or at least visited Spain frequently while they occurred. A dictatorship has been transformed, largely by its own servants and heirs, into a pluralistic, liberal parliamentary democracy. A uniform, highly centralized state has also begun to change into a diverse multinational one. And all this has happened without civil war, defeat by a foreign power, or revolutionary upheaval.

Some would argue that the lack of a social revolution and the fact that political power remained in the hands of heirs of the Franco regime meant that the transformation discussed here was superficial. The underlying premise of this book is that it was profound and important. It may be chic to dismiss the acquisition of "merely bourgeois formal liberties," but as anyone who experienced the Franco regime can testify, they are extremely important.

This book presents a narrative account of Spanish political life after the death of Franco. In a longer book, I might have chosen to start with the Civil War and to summarize the history of the Franco regime, but in an essay as brief as this it seemed to me preferable to begin simply with a snapshot of Spain as it existed at the dictator's death.

The aim of this essay is to examine how Spaniards founded a democracy after forty years of dictatorship. It is essentially a study in political change under the special conditions created by the demise of a very long-lived dictator. Changes in Spain have not been limited to the political sphere, but for the purposes of this book, social, cultural, and economic affairs are important only insofar as they impinge on the political process. Similarly, I touch on Spanish foreign relations only on those rare occasions when they must be taken into account to understand internal politics.

Most of the information in this book comes from the press and from interviews and conversations with scores of Spaniards, ranging from the then Prince Juan Carlos to taxi drivers, and from representatives of the ultra-leftist Workers' Revolutionary Organization (ORT) to ministers of the Franco regime. Conversations with Spanish and foreign journalists and with my colleagues both in Spain and in the United States have also proved helpful. I could not begin to make a complete list of the people whose insights and information have contributed to my understanding of Spain, but I do wish to thank them all. One person, however, must be mentioned specifically, Juan Linz of Yale University. I have benefited greatly from reading his pioneering studies of Spanish politics and from conversing with him. I wish here to acknowledge my debts and express my gratitude to him.

Since this study is based primarily on personal conversations and observations and on press articles, I have not provided footnotes. Chapter 2 relies more heavily on traditional academic sources, which are listed in my article cited at the beginning of that chapter.

At various times during the preparation of this book, Lee Cancio, Chip Morse, Diana Miller, and Roland Knaut served as my research assistants. Mr. Morse also did most of the work of preparing the index. Christopher Müller-Wille of the University of Chicago prepared the maps and charts. Cornelia Van Esso typed the final draft with awesome speed and efficiency. The Northwestern University Research Committee provided crucial financial support. To all of them, my thanks.

CONTENTS

		Page
PREFACE		vii
LIST OF TABLES, FIGURES, AND MAPS		xi
ABBREVIATIONS		xii

Chapter

1. SPAIN AT THE TIME OF FRANCO'S DEATH — 1

The Economy — 1
The Army — 4
The Church — 8
The Press and the Universities — 9
The Labor Movement and the Business Community — 11
Official Political Life — 13
Public Opinion and Political Groups — 16
Conclusion — 20

2. REGIONALISM — 21

Catalonia — 21
Historical Roots of Catalan Regionalism — 25
The Basque Country — 28
Historical Roots of Basque Regionalism — 32
Characteristics of Catalan and Basque Regionalism — 34

3. FROM FRANCO'S DEATH TO THE REFERENDUM — 36

The First Government of the Monarchy — 36
Arias's Reform — 40
President Suárez — 44
Political Reform — 50

4. FROM THE REFERENDUM TO THE
   JUNE 1977 ELECTIONS — 54

The Electoral Law — 55
The Legalization of Parties and the Amnesty — 56
Public Order — 60
Party Formation and the Electoral Campaign — 62
The Elections — 71

Chapter		Page
5.	AFTER THE ELECTIONS	81
	The Second Suarez Government	81
	Public Order	83
	Catalonia: The Return of Tarradellas	84
	The Basque Country	86
	Emergency Economic Measures	87
	The September Crisis	88
	Toward Catalan and Basque Autonomy and Amnesty	90
	The Moncloa Pact	91
	Municipal Elections and Trade Unions	94
	Regionalism	97
	Economics after the Moncloa Pact	102
	March Mini-Crisis	105
	The Basque Question and Public Order	106
	Economic Conditions	110
6.	THE CONSTITUTION	113
	The Drafting Process	113
	The Constitutional Referendum	118
	General Characteristics	125
	Parliamentary Monarchy	125
	Regional Autonomy	128
	Individual Rights and Public Liberties	130
	Constitutional Reform	133
7.	CONCLUSIONS	135
INDEX		142
ABOUT THE AUTHOR		151

LIST OF TABLES, FIGURES, AND MAPS

Table		Page
1.1	Active Population by Sectors, 1950–1974 (percentages)	2
1.2	GNP at Factor Cost by Origin, 1958–1975 (percentages)	2
1.3	Population by Size of Place of Residence, 1950–1970 (percentages)	3
1.4	Spain, Portugal, Greece, and Italy, 1974	5
1.5	Men under Arms and Military Expenditures, 1975	6
1.6	Students in Institutions of Higher Learning per 100,000 Inhabitants, 1970	10
2.1	Catalonia—Estimated Population and Population Density, 1975	22
2.2	Catalonia—Per Capita Income in 1971 and Rank among 50 Spanish Provinces	24
2.3	Catalonia—Immigration	24
2.4	The Basque Country—Estimated Population and Population Density, 1975	30
2.5	The Basque Country—Per Capita Income in 1971 and Rank among 50 Spanish Provinces	31
2.6	The Basque Country—Immigration	31
3.1	Results of the Referendum, December 1976	52
4.1	Election to Congress of Deputies, June 1977	73
4.2	Basque Country—Election to Congress of Deputies, June 1977	76
4.3	Catalonia—Election to Congress of Deputies, June 1977	78
6.1	Provincial Results of Referendum, December 1978	120
6.2	Catalonia: Referendum Results, December 1978	122
6.3	Basque Country: Referendum Results, December 1978	123
6.4	Basque Country: "Positive" Abstention in December 1978 Referendum	124

Figure		
4.1	Seats in the Congress of Deputies, June 1977	75
4.2	Basque Deputies, June 1977	77
4.3	Catalan Deputies, June 1977	79

Map		
2.1	Map of Catalonia	23
2.2	Map of the Basque Country	29
5.1	Map of Regions and Provinces, June 1977	101

ABBREVIATIONS

ANV	Acción Nacionalista Vasca (Basque Nationalist Action Party)
CD	Centro Democrática (Democratic Center)
CEOE	Confederación Española de Organizaciones Empresariales (Spanish Confederation of Business Organizations)
DC	Democracia Cristiana (Christian Democracy)
EC	Esquerra de Catalunya (Catalan Left)
EE	Euskadiko Ezquerra (Left of Euzkadi)
ESB	Euskal Sozialista Biltzarrea (Basque Socialist Party)
ETA	Euskadi ta Askatasuna (Basque Fatherland and Freedom)
FDI	Frente Democrático de Izquierdas (Left Democratic Front)
FPS	Federación de Partidos Socialistas (Federation of Socialist Parties)
GRAPO	Grupo de Resistencia Anti-Fascista Primero de Octubre (First of October Anti-Fascist Resistance Group)
MPAIAC	Movimiento Popular para la Autodeterminación e Independencia del Archipiélago Canario (Popular Movement for the Self-Determination and Independence of the Canarian Archipelago)
ORT	Organización Revolucionaria de Trabajadores (Workers' Revolutionary Organization)
PCE	Partido Comunista de España (Spanish Communist Party)
PEC	Pacte Democratic per Catalunya (Democratic Pact for Catalonia)
PNV	Partido Nacionalista Vasco (Basque Nationalist Party)
PP	Partido Popular (Popular Party)
PSOE	Partido Socialista Obrero Español (Spanish Socialist Workers' Party)
PSOE (h)	Partido Socialista Obrero Español (Histórico) (Historic Spanish Socialist Workers' Party)
PSP	Partido Socialista Popular (Popular Socialist Party)
PSUC	Partit Socialista Unificat de Catalunya (Unified Socialist Party of Catalonia)
SC	Socialistes de Catalunya (Socialists of Catalonia)
UCD	Unión del Centro Democrático (Center Democratic Union)
UDE	Unión Democrática Española (Spanish Democratic Union)
UPDE	Unión del Pueblo Español (Union of the Spanish People)
UGT	Unión General de Trabajadores (General Workers' Union)
UNE	Unión Nacional Española (Spanish National Union)

THE POLITICAL TRANSFORMATION OF SPAIN AFTER FRANCO

1

SPAIN AT THE TIME OF FRANCO'S DEATH

THE ECONOMY

A statement frequently attributed to the former Commissar of the Plan for Economic Development, Laureano López Rodó, asserted that Spain would be ready for democracy when it reached $2,000 a year per capita income. By that standard, at least, Franco's death was timely. As any frequent traveler to Spain could testify, the country had undergone a radical economic transformation in the decade and a half between 1960 and 1975. The story is well known and its details do not concern us here. This section will offer only a summary overview of the subject.

The 1974 GDP per capita stood at $2,446, up from roughly $300 in 1957 and $1,070 in 1971. The 1974 GNP was $85.5 billion, up 37 percent in real terms since 1969. Industrial production tripled between 1960 and 1970, and rose another 40 percent between 1970 and 1975. Growth was accompanied by a dramatic shift away from agriculture into industry and services, as is evident in the following two tables.

This process was naturally accompanied by rapid urbanization, as can be appreciated in Table 1.3. By 1970, Spain's two largest cities, Madrid and Barcelona, accounted for 14 percent of the country's population.

Geographic proximity and parallel histories of long-lived authoritarian regimes lead to frequent comparisons between Spain and Portugal,

---

Parts of Chapters 1–4 are based upon material from "Spain from Dictatorship to Democracy," in *International Affairs*, October 1977, pp. 615–30.

TABLE 1.1

Active Population by Sectors, 1950–1974
(percentages)

	Agriculture	Industry	Services
1950	50	26	25
1960	42	30	28
1970	25	38	37
1974	23	37	40

Source: INE, *Anuario estadístico de España 1977* (Madrid, INE, 1977), Table 1.1.3.2, p. 53. OECD, *Economic Surveys. Spain* (Paris, OECD, 1977).

TABLE 1.2

GNP at Factor Cost by Origin, 1958–1975
(percentages)

	Agriculture	Industry	Services
1958	27	31	42
1965	19	35	46
1970	13	36	51
1975	9	39	52

Source: OECD, *National Accounts Statistics. Expenditure, Product and Income 1955–64* (Paris, OECD, 1964), p. 140. OECD, *National Accounts of OECD Countries 1960–1970* (Paris, OECD [1972]), p. 266. OECD, *National Accounts of OECD Countries 1976* (Paris, OECD, n.d.), Vol. II, p. 288.

TABLE 1.3

Population by Size of Place of Residence, 1950–1970 (percentages)

	Less Than 10,000	10,000– 49,999	50,000– 99,999	100,000– 199,999	200,000– and up
1950	63	14	5	3	15
1960	54	13	10	6	18
1970	44	14	7	10	24

Source: Estudios sociológicos sobre la situación social de España, 1975, Editorial Euramérica, Madrid, 1976, p. 94.

but the two countries are economically dissimilar. Spain is richer, more developed, and much larger than her neighbor. In many ways she is closer to Greece and even to Italy than to Portugal, as can be seen in Table 1.4.

Spanish economic growth during the 1960s and early 1970s benefited from the generally prosperous conditions of the Western economy and depended heavily on tourism, worker remittances, and foreign investment. Nonetheless, in the words of an OECD report: "By comparison with the experience of other member countries, the Spanish economy weathered both the oil crisis and the aftershock of the world recession, reasonably well. In 1975 it was one of the few countries not to register a year-on-year fall in activity."* Between 1971 and 1976 GNP grew at an average annual rate of 4.9 percent, less than Greece, Turkey, and Japan but higher than any other OECD country. The growth of per capita income, at an annual rate of 3.9 percent, was exceeded only in Greece and Turkey.

All this is not to say that 1975 was a good year. Spain was not buffeted as hard as some of her neighbors, but, again in the words of the OECD report, it "was probably the worst year Spain had had, in terms of declining activity and rising unemployment, since 1959." If the situation was not as serious as in many other countries, it was in part because Franco's last government deliberately chose inflation rather than stagnation and unemployment. This decision would condition events in Spain during the months following the Caudillo's death.

THE ARMY

The army was the institution most frequently mentioned in discussions of Spanish politics during the Franco era. According to one survey, in 1973 Spaniards of all ages, social groups, and educational levels considered it the most powerful group in their country's political life. The Spanish armed forces, however, do not bulk extraordinarily large in number of men under arms nor in percentage of government expenditures, as can be seen in Table 1.5.

Considering that it was born of a civil war and led by a general, the Franco regime allowed the army a surprisingly limited role in day-to-day political life. In recent years, military men, except for Admiral Luis Carrero Blanco, rarely occupied cabinet posts other than military ones. In the military academies, professional attitudes and interests were fostered and active interest in politics discouraged. Officers were expected to be

---

*OECD, *Economic Surveys, Spain 1976* (OECD, Paris, 1976), p. 5.

TABLE 1.4

Spain, Portugal, Greece, and Italy, 1974

Item	Spain	Portugal	Greece	Italy
Population (thousands)	35,219	9,448	9,046	55,812
Active Population In:				
Agriculture (%)	23.1	28.2	36.2	16.6
Industry (%)	37.2	33.6	27.8	44.1
Services (%)	39.7	38.2	36.0	39.3
Total GDP in US $ Billions	85.50	13.32	19.17	149.81
GDP per Capita in US $	2,446	1,517	2,139	2,706
Private Consumption per Capita in US $	1,444	1,089	1,517	1,782
Passenger Cars: per 1,000 Inhabitants	109	90	39	243
Telephones: per 1,000 Inhabitants	181	109	187	229
Access to Higher Education: Percentage of Relevant Age Group	27.1	9.8	—	27.9
Infant Mortality	13.6	44.8	23.9	22.6

Source: OECD, *Economic Surveys, Spain 1977* (OECD, Paris, 1977), Annex "Basic Statistics: International Comparisons."

TABLE 1.5

Men under Arms and Military Expenditures, 1975

	Armed Forces per 1,000 Population	Per Capita Expenditures in 1974 Dollars	Military Expenditure as Percent of GNP
Spain	10.50	72	3.0
Austria	6.63	43	1.0
Denmark	6.91	155	2.6
France	10.87	197	4.0
Germany	7.98	216	3.6
Greece	21.21	145	6.3
Italy	8.95	73	2.8
Norway	8.73	193	3.3
Portugal	25.50	108	7.6
Turkey	11.25	36	4.5

Source: U.S. Arms Control and Disarmament Agency, *World Military Expenditures and Arms Transfers, 1966–75* (The Agency, Washington, D.C., 1977), Table II, pp. 19–55.

loyal to Franco, and to the principles of the National Movement, but not to take a direct or active part in political life. These policies produced a professionalized officer corps, anxious to maintain its identity and interests, by and large conservative in its opinions, but with little contact with or interest in day-to-day politics.

By the 1970s, Spain's social and educational development made it difficult if not impossible for the armed forces to believe in good faith that they constituted the trained elite of the country, as was the case in Peru or Portugal. Economic development had been accompanied by increasing levels of education and by the rise of a relatively modern and effective bureaucracy and managerial class. Most military leaders recognized that they lacked the training and experience necessary to run a complex economic and political system, and they were not anxious to assume direct political responsibilities.

By the time of Franco's death, most generals with command of troops were men who had graduated from the military academies after the Civil War. The last of the "blue generals," those personally committed to the historical Falange, were retired and had no political influence. Among the generals and colonels, conservatives still predominated, but few were passionately committed to maintaining the regime's institutions intact, and many were favorably disposed toward at least some mild gradual reform.

The best-known "liberal" among the military, Lieutenant General Manuel Díaz Alegría, who was largely responsible for preventing harsher measures in the wake of the assassination of Admiral Carrero Blanco, had been dismissed in 1974 under pressure from the ultras, but he still enjoyed considerable prestige both in the army and among the general public.

The existence of the leftist Spanish Military Union (UME), nine of whose members were arrested in July 1975, is no sign that there was in the Spanish army anything even remotely comparable to the left-wing groups that came to dominate the Portuguese army. Spanish officers were discontented about their pay and promotions, and anxious for more funds with which to modernize their forces, but they had undergone no radicalizing experience like that of the Portuguese army in Africa and remained firmly anchored in the center and right of the political spectrum.

The army's monopoly of substantial armed strength and the almost universal conviction that it would use force if necessary, made it a critical factor in determining the parameters within which other political groups could maneuver. No responsible government or opposition figure was likely to take steps or to make proposals which seemed destined to provoke direct army intervention.

The army's influence on politics was not usually exercised, of course, through threats of direct intervention, but conservative members of the armed forces in the Council of the Realm, the Cortes, and the cabinet were influential to the degree that they appeared to express not only their own opinions but those of their respective services. They frequently represented a real obstacle to reform, and on other occasions civilian politicians who professed to favor change but opposed concrete reforms, used the excuse of army opposition to hide their own reluctance to see fundamental changes instituted.

Some attention must also be paid to the paramilitary Civil Guard and to the Armed Police. The Civil Guard, with some 60,000 men, is responsible for policing all rural areas, for highway traffic, and control of ports and frontiers. It is commanded by a lieutenant general of the army. Members of the Civil Guard are never assigned to their home provinces, and are generally discouraged from making contact with the local population. Particularly in the rural areas of the Basque country, the patrols of the Civil Guard are greeted with suspicion and hostility and regarded as the chief repressive arm of the regime. The 20,000 members of the militarized Armed Police, known as *grises* from their gray uniforms, are responsible, together with the General Police Corps, for policing all population centers of more than 30,000 inhabitants. The tradition of strict obedience to authority makes both the Civil Guard and the Armed Police formidable resources in the government's hands.

THE CHURCH

After the bitter persecution it underwent in the Republican zone during the Civil War, the Church was grateful for Franco's protection. His regime helped rebuild ruined seminaries, churches, and convents, and gave the Church a leading role in education. In return, especially during the years immediately following the Civil War, members of the hierarchy and leaders of Catholic associations were often lavish in their praise of Franco and his regime. The Vatican, for its part, maintained close relations with the Spanish government and for years considered the 1953 concordat with Spain a model for treaties governing church-state relations in Catholic countries.

During the last decade of the Franco regime, all of this changed so sharply that by 1974 the Church's influence certainly favored change more than continuity. The Second Vatican Council's stress on the dignity of the human person and on respect for personal liberty raised many difficult questions about supporting the Franco regime. Its pronouncements on religious liberty, with their stress on government respect for religious freedom rather than on close church-state relations, made the arrangements between Madrid and the Vatican seem antiquated if not embarrassing.

In the mid-sixties, a growing belief that too close an association with the Franco regime would prove disadvantageous following the Generalissimo's death, moved the Vatican to appoint a new generation of bishops critical of the social and political situation of their country. Ten years later, these younger bishops held a majority in the Episcopal Conference and had passed frequent statements condemning various aspects of the Franco regime. They called not only for amnesty and reconciliation, but for concrete reforms in Spanish political life.

The changes of orientation of the younger clergy were even more pronounced. A significant proportion was favorable to some form of socialism or social democracy and many more criticized the Franco regime. The number of priests involved in working-class movements was relatively small, but they were very influential and attracted much attention. Support for regional movements in the Basque country and Catalonia was very widespread among the clergy, who were in many cases active organizers of regional groups.

THE PRESS AND THE UNIVERSITIES

The Franco regime was based on the denial of open conflict and on management through behind-the-scenes manipulation by the Caudillo. With the passage of years it has become necessary, however, to admit growing, if still severely limited, public expression of the conflict that actually existed within the society.

During the first twenty-five years of Franco's reign, prior censorship of all printed material guaranteed that newspapers and magazines would adhere to the government's line on all questions. Criticism of official policy as well as discussion of possible alternative approaches was totally banned.

In 1966 a new press law prepared by the Minister of Information, Manuel Fraga Irribarne, abolished censorship, opening the first breach in this wall. The new law took a great step forward by recognizing the right of freedom of expression in the press, but it immediately qualified this right by requiring respect for the principles of the National Movement and for "institutions and persons in expressing criticism of public and administrative action."

Under the new law, newspapers became much more interesting and informative. Three new Madrid dailies introduced Spain to a more modern and independent form of journalism. The Ministry of Information, under Fraga's direction, however, made full use of the broad discretionary powers granted to it by the law to control and harrass journalists and publications who incurred its displeasure. By 1971, all three new papers had been destroyed by administrative sanctions. The last to go was *Madrid*, whose editor, Rafael Calvo Serrer, went into exile in France when his paper was finally closed down.

The establishment of the Arias government and the naming of Pío Cabanillas as Minister of Information in January 1974 greatly accelerated the pace of change. No new legislation was introduced, but journalists were quick to perceive that the new minister was willing to allow far more criticism than any of his predecessors. Certain topics remained taboo. No criticism of General Franco was tolerated (or even attempted), and excessive frankness in discussing government activities could still lead to sanctions. Nonetheless, the change in tone of the Spanish press was startling to anyone accustomed to its tame uniformity in the past. Newspapers and magazines spoke freely of the "crisis of the regime" and discussed the government's "lack of any coherent policy." Shortly after President Arias's first televised press conference, in itself an indication of a new tone, a Madrid daily published the results of a poll which indicated that over a fourth of the population had found the press conference disappointing or very disappointing, and that more than half described the President of the Government's answers as evasive or not very clear. Most newspapers established fixed pages or sections for information about strikes and reported freely on other illegal political and labor activities. The situation of the press at Franco's death was, thus, a far cry from that of a decade earlier.

In 1976, a member of the Cortes described the Spanish universities as a "Marxist bunker." This statement is undoubtedly exaggerated, but it does reflect the fact that during the final decades of the Franco regime the universities grew steadily more radical and became a significant factor in the strength of the political left.

Between 1960 and 1970 the number of students enrolled in Spanish universities and other institutions of higher learning grew 167 percent, from 77,000 to 205,000. (See Table 1.6.) In 1970, 57.2 percent of the students came from families of professionals, executives, administrators, and businessmen; 29.2 percent came from families of members of the armed forces, employees, shopkeepers, craftsmen, and service personnel; and 13.5 percent from working-class families.

TABLE 1.6

Students in Institutions of Higher Learning— per 100,000 Inhabitants, 1970

Country	Number
Spain	653
Belgium	776
France	1,211
Germany	839
Italy	1,280
Mexico	488
Portugal	520
Venezuela	718

Source: Calculated from UNESCO, *Statistical Yearbook, 1972* (Paris, UNESCO, 1973), pp. 19–23 and 325–39.

Spanish universities faced serious problems of lack of staff and facilities. Classrooms and laboratories were inadequate, and libraries in most cases virtually nonexistent. A high proportion of the faculty was made up of professors on one-year contracts; their pay was low and their situation was extremely precarious. Among both faculty and students, Marxism and other left-wing ideologies were strong, particularly in the social sciences and humanities. The internal difficulties of the university contributed to the strength of left-wing ideologies and made for a discontented mass of students who could easily be mobilized for protests and demonstrations in which purely university questions and more general political ones tended to overlap.

THE LABOR MOVEMENT AND
THE BUSINESS COMMUNITY

The Franco regime's efforts to avoid labor conflicts proved more unsuccessful over the long run than its attempts to control the press. The state-controlled syndicates were the only legally recognized labor organizations in Spain. Modeled on Italian and German fascist patterns, they theoretically included and represented everyone from factory owners to workers. State control was supposed to make them responsive not to the needs of one group or another, but to the superior requirements of the entire community.

During the first quarter century of the regime's existence, the vertical syndicates were highly successful in controlling the labor market. Strikes were infrequent and unsuccessful. Efforts to organize worker resistance, often attempted by the Communist Party, led only to frustration and long jail sentences. The official syndicates generally served to discipline labor rather than to represent its interests, although they did win almost absolute job security for their members as well as a steadily increasing package of benefits.

Over time, the frustration of the workers with the failure of their supposed representatives to pursue their interests led to a search for alternative forms of organization. During a strike in the La Camucha mine in Asturias in 1956, an ad hoc strike committee was organized with the name of *Comisión obrera* or Workers' Commission. In 1962–64, numerous similar committees were formed in other mines. At first their activities were strictly limited to leading and negotiating the settlement of strikes, all of which were illegal, but gradually the committees became permanent bodies.

The organizers of these committees came from diverse political backgrounds and included many Catholics and a number of Falangists; Communists were not particularly prominent among the initial organizers. By the time the first Madrid meeting of the Workers' Commissions was held in 1964, Communists had begun to be influential. By the time a national coordinating council with a central secretariat and eleven provincial councils had been set up in 1970, Communist influence had become dominant in many areas.

During the Second Republic, labor unions played a prominent role in Spanish politics, and the Italian experience suggested that they would do so again if Spain continued to evolve toward some form of political and social organization patterned on that of the Western European countries. Up to 1975, however, the working class showed relatively little interest in broader political questions. Instead, it centered its concerns on issues of wages, working conditions, benefits, and union organization. The depoliticization, which affected all elements of Spanish society during the Franco regime, seems to have been particularly profound among the members of the working class. A survey taken in late 1973 found that only 12 percent of workers could be classified as being "very interested" or "quite interested" in politics. During the following two years, interest in politics certainly increased, but most members of the working class still exhibited much more concern about the economic situation than about politics.

In 1974, although all strikes continued to be illegal, Spain ranked among the top five European countries in the number of workdays lost through strikes. During Franco's lifetime, the motives for most strikes were a mixture of economic demands and such others as elsewhere would have been considered purely labor questions, as for instance, the election of union officials. Broader political issues were of slight importance in most strikes. Workers backed attempts to call a general strike to "overthrow the dictatorship" much less enthusiastically than did students.

The number of strikes during the final years of the Franco regime is the most significant index of the success of the Workers' Commissions in organizing at the local factory level, where they often displaced the official *sindicatos* altogether. Industrialists began to negotiate directly with the Commissions despite legal prohibitions, since they alone could guarantee that a settlement would be recognized by the workers. The vast official union organization was still standing, but its base had entirely eroded away. In May 1975, faced with the demonstrated impossibility of repressing all strikes in a relatively highly industrialized economy, the government decided to acquiesce in the strike as a fact of life, although hedging it about with stringent controls.

The Spanish business community also changed radically during the last twenty years of the regime. By the time of Franco's death, it was the backbone of support for non-socialist liberalism. Its most important members had frequent and close contacts with Western Europe and with the United States and had absorbed more liberal political attitudes than the majority of the population. Especially among those engaged in large-scale businesses, the desire to enter the Common Market served to reinforce their convictions and to align them with the partisans of change. A 1973 survey showed that on questions of *political* reform—freedom of the press, political parties, elected government, etc.—business owners and managers were more liberal than any other occupational group of the population, with the exception of students. They also supported popular participation in government by a wider margin than any other group except students, and showed the highest index of interest in politics of any occupational group. On economic questions, not surprisingly, the majority of businessmen were favorable to free enterprise, although many said they leaned toward some form of social democracy. Fully 74 percent of the businessmen surveyed considered freedom to form labor unions desirable while only 19 percent were opposed.

OFFICIAL POLITICAL LIFE

The Franco regime continued, right down to the death of its founder, to be the outgrowth of victory in civil war, and consequently to divide the population into victors and vanquished. Some of the bitterness had dissipated with the passage of time and the number of political prisoners had declined from 250,000 or more in 1940 to under 1,000. But the regime continued to base its legitimacy on victory in war and on Franco's constituent powers as the leader of the victorious coalition. Juan Carlos's position as future king was based not on dynastic considerations, which would have dictated that his father, Don Juan de Borbón, should occupy the throne, but rather on Franco's designation. It is perhaps for this reason that the question of amnesty would loom so large on the political horizon immediately after Franco's death. The number of people directly affected was not large, roughly two per 100,000 of the population, but the symbolic importance of amnesty as an act of reconciliation putting a final end to the Civil War cannot be measured in numerical terms.

The regime continued to be a personal one-man dictatorship. Franco relinquished control over the day-to-day affairs of government during the regime's last years, but final power definitely remained in his hands, and he was the source of legitimacy for both government and administration.

The regime which Franco established during the Civil War shared with the Fascist regimes of the interwar years an anti-liberal, anti-Communist policy and a highly authoritarian character, but was distinguished from them by its marked reluctance to mobilize the population politically. General Franco preferred political apathy to enthusiasm. Except in unusual circumstances, his regime made no attempt to elicit mass support, rather preferring passive acceptance of its decrees.

Francoism was not an ideology but a personal system of government, based on the groups that formed the victorious coalition during the war, and centered around their commanding general. Its legitimacy, at first based almost entirely on victory in war, later was strengthened by prolonged peace and order, and ultimately by economic development. The regime never had a fully elaborated or sharply defined ideology, beyond opposition to liberalism and communism, and rejection of the Second Republic and its politics. Especially in the years immediately following the Civil War, all of this was clothed in corporativist garb borrowed from Italian Fascism and German National Socialism as well as from the early Catholic corporativist tradition; but this ideology won only limited acceptance from the population and played only a slight role in the stability of the regime. What little ideological legitimacy it lent the regime in its early years was seriously eroded by the defeat of the Fascist powers in World War II and later by Catholic shifts away from corporativism.

The Falange, founded by José Antonio Primo de Rivera, was still a miniscule organization when the Spanish Civil War broke out in 1936. It played no significant part in the planning or execution of the original uprising, but grew very quickly during the early months of the war. In March 1936, Franco fused it with the political organization of the conservative Carlist monarchists, the Carlist communion, to form the Falange Española Tradicionalista y de las Jons, which became in theory the Spanish state party, and was in fact the only permitted political organization.

Despite its theoretical position of dominance, the Falange never became, even in its most prosperous period during World War II, an exclusive vehicle of political participation and promotion of elites. By the 1950s it played only a secondary role in the recruitment of leaders, and had little control over the distribution of the social benefits provided by the state. Most successful politicians were nominal members of the Falange, but only a minority owed their success to identification with it.

Especially after 1957, the Falange became less and less important as a route to power and influence, although many aspirants to a political career still began working during their university days in the official student syndicate, S.E.U. From there they went on to the syndicates, the Ministry of the Interior, or one of the other ministries. Their identification with the historic Falange and its ideology was weak or nonexistent. At least those who reached the upper levels of government owed their primary loyalty to Franco, not to the Falange, and were expected to collaborate with men drawn from the other "political families" of the regime.

In 1966, the Falange ceased to be even theoretically a state party, and was transformed into an amorphous "National Movement." This evolution meant that at Franco's death the Falange did not constitute a clearly defined party and did not enjoy the power or prestige of the state parties in other authoritarian regimes.

Franco's governments habitually included elements of all the major groups that supported the regime. Large parts of the population were systematically excluded from any active role in politics, but a certain limited pluralism always existed among the various interests in the coalition that won the Civil War. Franco watchers classified his "governments" in terms of the relative weight of Falangists, Alphonsine monarchists, members of the Catholic Action, and Carlists.

In recent years, "technocrats" grouped around Laureano López Rodó also figured prominently in Franco's cabinets. This group was sometimes identified with Opus Dei, the Catholic lay association to which López Rodó belonged. Opus Dei, however, always protested against the use of its name in this context, pointing out that its members held diverse political views quite independent of their membership in the organization. This was clear enough at the time. One Opus Dei member, for instance, published in the early seventies a daily, *Madrid*, whose criticism of the regime led the government to shut it down in 1971. With the legalization of political parties, the political diversity of Opus Dei members has become even more evident. López Rodó and his "technocratic" associates undoubtedly formed a coherent political group, but it cannot be identified with Opus Dei.

Ministers did not enter Franco's government as representatives of the groups to which they belonged, but solely by virtue of Franco's choice, and they were expected to put aside all other loyalties if they came into conflict with their primary loyalty to Franco himself. In this sense the terms "crisis" and "new government" applied to the Franco period are misleading. The entire forty-year Franco period saw only one "government," the "Franco government," which was renewed from time to time with the introduction of new faces, but which did not undergo crises and changes similar to those of governments of countries with representative parliaments.

Increasingly in recent years, most appointments to cabinet and subcabinet level posts were made from the ranks of the bureaucracy. The typical career pattern of Franco's ministers began with a brilliant university record, followed by entrance into one of the great privileged corps of government functionaries—lawyers of the state, economists of the state, university professors, etc.—and gradual advance through the bureaucracy to the level of Director General. The cabinet formed by Arias after the assassination of Admiral Carrero Blanco in January 1974 represents the final step in this dominance of upper-level functionaries in Spanish politics. Almost all its ministers had served previously as Directors General or in other major administrative posts.

As outlined above, over the course of the years the regime came to allow greater expression of contrasting opinions and interests, but it permitted scarcely any increase in participation. It established no institutional channels for influencing government policy other than elections of the "family" representatives to the Cortes, whose authority was severely limited. Politics continued to be the preserve of an elite, whose decisions were made behind closed doors without public debate and with no mechanisms for public input. Only those sectors which had traditionally been represented in Franco's governments had any publicly recognized influence on decisions. Others could, and in fact did influence policy, but they had no institutional access to government and were forced in many cases to rely on strikes and other illegal activities to make themselves heard.

PUBLIC OPINION AND POLITICAL GROUPS

By the time of Franco's death, a large and vocal segment of Spanish opinion had come to reject altogether the characteristic features of his regime. In a country in which 70 percent of the population was under forty years of age and had no memories at all of the Civil War, victory over the Republic was no longer an acceptable claim to power. The children of the victors had long since begun to feel uncomfortable with the situation and many were calling loudly for a government based on the recognition of popular sovereignty.

The system of one-man rule ceased to be viable with the Caudillo's death. Franco himself had been very careful to see that no one else in the country developed an independent base of power and prestige. At the first sign that a minister was beginning to enjoy a certain amount of popularity in his own right, he became a likely candidate for replacement in the next change of personnel. Probably the best known and most popular figure at Franco's death was the then ambassador to London, Manuel Fraga Irribarne, but he had no very large following, no independent and organized source of power. One of the few things that could be predicted with some assurance at Franco's death was that no one would inherit power even approaching that which the Caudillo had wielded during his long lifetime. Whatever the outcome of the difficult transition to post-Francoism, it would not include a return to one-man rule of the type Franco had exercised.

Whether post-Franco Spain would provide for a larger degree of political participation by its citizens was open to question, but clearly many Spaniards wanted a chance to take part in their country's political life. Even those groups that had benefited most conspicuously from the government's policies were often vocal in their demands for a greater and more direct voice in government, through open elections. In some cases these demands were motivated by opportunism and an awareness that flexibility was going to be necessary to preserve acquired positions. In many others, however, they seem to have reflected a genuine desire for forms of government closer to the Western European norm.

Over the two decades prior to Franco's death, Spain had been in increasingly close contact with her European neighbors through trade, tourism, cultural interchange, etc. Most Spaniards had gradually come to judge their country by the standards prevalent in Western Europe and to long for comparable institutions. The Spanish right continued to denounce, as it had since the time of the French Revolution, those who wished to "copy" other countries, but many Spaniards wished to do precisely that. In a national survey conducted in December 1975, 42.2 percent of those polled and 51.7 percent of those expressing an opinion said they favored making the changes necessary to bring the Spanish system into line with that of the democratic countries of Western Europe.

It is important for the country's political future that a majority of Spaniards look to the more advanced countries of Western Europe, not Portugal or Greece, much less Latin America or other areas of the Third World, when searching for political models. Even before Franco's death, the desire to build a stable democratic system had become an important factor in Spanish politics.

After the assassination of Admiral Carrero Blanco on December 20, 1973, Franco named Carlos Arias Navarro President of the Government. Arias shared Franco's aversion to party politics, but realized the transition at Franco's death would be much easier if the country had been prepared beforehand. On February 12, 1974 he made an important policy speech that seemed to herald a new spirit in Spanish politics. The "spirit of February 12" was to be one of "opening up" the country, or *apertura*.

In terms of legislation the results of the new spirit were meager. Arias promised to allow the creation not of political *parties* (a term General Franco would never have accepted), but of political *associations*, foreseen already in the legislation of the National Movement. The events of the succeeding months were dominated by a tug-of-war between ultra-conservatives and moderates within the regime. By putting his prestige on the line, Arias did manage to obtain a statute of political associations, but the law as finally approved was hedged about with such restrictions that it was stillborn. It vested control of any associations which might be formed in the Council of the National Movement, the chief stronghold of hard-line Falangists, and required all associations to pledge explicit adherence to the principles of the National Movement. Under such conditions, even the most moderate opposition groups refused to participate. The only associations which were formed were led by supporters of the regime, such as Gonzalo Fernández de la Mora of the Spanish National Union (UNE), and Adolfo Suárez of the Union of the Spanish People (UDPE).

Arias's February 12 speech introduced into Spain's political vocabulary a new term, *aperturistas,* to designate men committed to greater openness in the political system but willing to work from within and convinced that it was desirable, or at least inevitable, that reform should come as a concession of the government rather than as a result of a constituent process born of free elections. The *aperturistas* constituted not a group but a relatively broad category which included members of a number of different formal groupings. They had no one organ of opinion, no meeting place, and no single organization. What united them was their belief in reform from above, joined to their position on the fringes of, but still within, the Franco regime during its closing period.

The two best known *aperturistas* were José María de Areilza and Manual Fraga Irribarne. Areilza, a banker and diplomat, former ambassador to Washington and Paris, advocated a policy of bringing Spain into Europe. A long-term liberal monarchist, he campaigned actively for a more liberal, democratic political system.

Fraga had served as Franco's Minister of Information and Tourism from 1962 to 1969. He first established his credentials as a partisan of reform thanks to the press law of 1967, although his administration of it reflected the contradictions that characterized this authoritarian "liberal." During the closing months of the Franco regime, even Fraga's warmest supporters, of whom he had many, admitted that he was by temperament highly authoritarian, but they vigorously defended the sincerity of his commitment to democracy. This was, to a greater or lesser degree, the inherent contradiction of the entire group of *aperturistas* who favored change but wanted to effect it themselves, defended liberty but were willing to see it granted only according to their own timetable.and under their own conditions.

To the left of the *aperturistas* stood a number of ill-defined "semi-legal and alegal" opposition groups that enjoyed no legal standing but, as Juan Linz has pointed out, were permitted by the authorities to carry out some activities without serious hindrance. They existed more as shades of opinions than as organized and structured groups. The exact form they had at the time of Franco's death is unimportant for our purposes. In later chapters we will see them take shape more clearly as Liberals, Christian Democrats, and Social Democrats.

The Socialists, who would play such an important role less than two years later, were still a negligible quantity in Spanish politics at Franco's death. Many people held Socialist opinions, but inside Spain the party's organization was virtually nonexistent.

Organized left-wing opposition to the Franco regime was limited almost exclusively to the Communist Party (PCE). The Spanish Communist Party's clandestine organization, its international support, and the skill and determination of its leadership made it possible for it to survive the long years of the Franco dictatorship, and to keep alive at least a minimal organization within Spain. During those years, the government's tendency to attack as "communist" all forms of left-wing opposition helped the PCE to develop its image as the only source of effective opposition, thus attracting to itself many opponents of the regime who felt little enthusiasm for its ideology. Many Christians who initially rejected the party for its doctrinaire materialism gradually came to collaborate with it. Some accepted all or a large part of its ideology, which they defended as compatible with their Christian beliefs, while others merely opted in favor of political collaboration with the party while continuing to reject its ideology. In the final years of the regime, the appearance of Maoist groups on its left embarrassed the Communist Party, but these groups were both too small and too extremist to seriously diminish the PCE's appeal as the most important opposition group.

Since 1960 the Secretary General of the PCE has been Santiago Carrillo. Born in Asturias in 1916, the son of a Socialist Union organizer, Carrillo worked as a typographer and was active in the Socialist Youth Organization, whose fusion with the Communist Party he helped arrange just before the outbreak of the Civil War. In 1936, he formally joined the PCE, and the following year he became a member of its central committee.

Carrillo's rise to power within the party was closely associated with the changes that followed on Stalin's death. Long an advocate of popular front tactics, Carrillo based the party's policies on the supposition that a successful violent revolution in Spain was unlikely and that the PCE needed to collaborate with all opposition groups and exploit all legal or tolerated means to promote subversion. Since the Sixth Party Congress in 1960, the PCE welcomed the collaboration of "progressive" Catholics and other members of the opposition. In 1968 this tactic was officially designated the *pacto para la libertad*, or "pact for liberty."

Unlike his Portuguese counterpart, Alvaro Cunhal, Carrillo repeatedly declared his faith in democratic government, and his commitment to majority rule. He also stressed the PCE's independence from Moscow, and sharply criticized the Soviet invasion of Czechoslovakia in 1968. Differences over this point caused a schism in the party, with the pro-Moscow faction splitting off under the leadership of the Civil War General Enrique Lister.

Most outside observers were convinced that the PCE was in fact quite independent of Moscow. Within Spain, however, many vigorously rejected this view. For most of the older generation, and for many younger people as well, the image of the PCE was fixed during the Civil War. It would be difficult to overestimate the distrust and hatred with which the Spanish right viewed the party. The experience of Eastern Europe after World War II and of the countries of the Third World that have come under Communist control in recent years were repeatedly adduced as proof of the assertion that the PCE's declarations of democratic faith were tactical and would not be respected should it ever see itself in a position of authority.

As Franco's proximate demise became more and more likely, the PCE under Carrillo's leadership made another attempt to gain acceptance and legitimacy by uniting with other opposition forces. On July 30, 1974, Carrillo and Rafael Calvo Serer, the exiled former editor of *Madrid*, announced the creation of *Junta Democrática* in Paris. Its manifesto called for a broad series of reforms beginning with an amnesty for all political offenders and including a free press, the right to strike and organize trade unions, elections, and entry into the EC. The *Junta* failed to attract the broad support Carrillo had hoped for. Neither the extreme left nor the Spanish Socialist Workers' Party (PSOE) was willing to join. Nonetheless, the *Junta* would prove a useful instrument since the collaboration of the conservative Calvo Serer helped to dispel the fear of the PCE.

CONCLUSION

The economic changes sketched in the first section of this chapter were too obvious to escape notice. It can be argued that they occurred despite the government's policies, as a result of the general European economic boom and the influx of money from tourists and worker re-mittances, but the fact of sweeping change cannot be denied. Critics of the Franco regime, and foreign journalists who flew into Madrid for a few days to write their stories, did, however, frequently ignore many of the other changes we have outlined in the subsequent sections. Politically, they said, nothing had really changed.

Although the fact that Franco remained at the head of the one-man authoritarian regime served to give color to this assertion, it is funda-mentally misleading. If behind the façade of the National Movement and the reality of Franco's personal power, profound changes had not taken place, the course of Spanish politics after Franco's death would surely have been very different. Precisely because the regime had been forced to tolerate a freer press and labor unions, and because it had lost the active support of the Church, the universities, and parts of the business com-munity, the kinds of changes we will examine in this book could take place. Had the regime been in 1975 what it was in 1955 or even 1965, the sequence of events we will explore could not have taken place as it did. Spain could go from the principles of the National Movement to a consti-tution providing for liberal parliamentary democracy in only three years and without a revolution only because in the decade and a half preceding the death of the dictator, profound changes had taken place in the social and political as well as economic structure of the nation.

2

REGIONALISM

The preceding chapter dealt with Spain as if it were a single homogeneous whole, without any significant regional differences. This is, of course, far from being the case. The country exhibits such marked regional characteristics that finding a way to accommodate them has proved to be one of the most critical and intractable problems facing Spanish political leaders. The future success or failure of Spain's political transformation is closely tied to the efforts being made to change a centralist state into a multinational one.

By 1978 virtually every part of Spain, including Castile, had witnessed demonstrations in favor of regional autonomy, and most regions had received a statute of pre-autonomy. Prior to Franco's death, however, only Catalonia, the Basque country, Galicia, and the Canary Islands had regional nationalist movements worthy of mention. Of these four, the first two were by far the most important, and this chapter will confine itself to examining them.

CATALONIA

The Catalan region in northeastern Spain comprises the provinces of Barcelona, Gerona, Lérida, and Tarragona, and has a population of

---

This chapter is a modified version of my essay "Regional Challenges to the Nation-State: The Case of Spain," published in *The State in Europe*, Arthur Cyr, ed. (Chicago: Chicago Council on Foreign Relations, 1977), pp. 43–65. Readers are referred to it for references to the literature.

approximately 5.7 million (see Map 2.1 and Table 2.1). This amounts to 16 percent of Spain's 35.5 million inhabitants, and makes Catalonia larger than Denmark, Finland, Norway, Ireland, or Israel. The four provinces which make up the region cover a total of 32,000 km², but the population is concentrated in the city of Barcelona, whose estimated 1.8 million inhabitants in 1975 constituted 32 percent of the regional total.

Catalonia ranks among the wealthiest areas in Spain. Even in its poorest province, Tarragona, per capita income was ten percent above the national average in 1971. Barcelona's high per capita income and large population make its total income the highest of any Spanish province. In 1971 its 388 billion pesetas amounted to 16 percent of the national total. Taken together, the four Catalan provinces accounted for 20 percent of Spain's GNP in 1971 (Table 2.2).

Economic prosperity and demand for labor have produced a strong current of immigration into Catalonia during most of this century. By 1950, people born in other provinces made up 37.8 percent of the population of the province of Barcelona. During the economic boom of the 1960s, the influx of immigrants from other regions of Spain was particularly strong. Immigration has diluted the native Catalan population and has contributed to the decline in the percentage of speakers of the language, although some assimilation has taken place (Table 2.3).

The linguistic basis for Catalan nationalism is strong. Eighty-four percent of the population is familiar with the language, and 97 percent of those born in the region speak Catalan. Eighty-six percent of native Catalans report that they usually speak Catalan at home and over half speak it regularly at work. Unlike Basque, it is a language of culture, with

TABLE 2.1

Catalonia—Estimated Population and Population Density, 1975

Province	Population	Area in Km²	Population per Km²
Barcelona	4,472,963	7,733	578
Gerona	441,667	5,886	75
Lérida	349,462	12,028	29
Tarragona	467,438	6,283	74
Total	5,701,540	31,930	179*

*Average population per km².
Source: INE, *España 1977, Anuario Estadístico* (Madrid, INE, 1977), pp. 9 and 455.

MAP 2.1

Map of Catalonia

Source: Confederación española de Cajas de Ahorres, *España. Atlas e Indices de sus Terminos Municipales* (Madrid, la Confederación, 1969).

TABLE 2.2

Catalonia—Per Capita Income in 1971 and Rank among 50 Spanish Provinces

Province	Per Capita Income in Pesetas	Index (Spanish National Average = 100)	Rank 1971
Barcelona	97,347	137.57	5
Gerona	87,248	123.30	7
Lérida	79,022	111.67	10
Tarragona	77,690	109.79	11

Source: Tamames, *Introducción a la economía española*. 9th ed. (Madrid, Alianza Editorial, 1974), pp. 422–23.

TABLE 2.3

Catalonia—Immigration*

Province	Number of Persons	Percent of Population of More than Ten Years of Age
Barcelona	582,169	18
Gerona	30,717	9
Lérida	17,359	6
Tarragona	35,483	10
Catalonia	665,728	15.8

*Population of more than ten years of age registered in the province in the 1970 census who were registered in a province of a different region in the 1960 census.
Source: Calculated from *Estudios sociológicos sobre la situación social de España 1975* (Madrid, Editorial Euramérica, 1976), Table VII.5, pp. 74–79.

an important literature and a significant number of scientific works published. Catalan is important for social and economic success in the region.

Affective identification with Catalonia is strong and widespread. In a survey conducted in 1975, 56.4 percent of the respondents in Catalonia said that they thought of themselves primarily as Catalans, whereas 37.7 percent thought of themselves primarily as Spanish. This study does not distinguish between rural and urban respondents, but earlier surveys show that in Catalonia regional identification is nearly as strong in large metropolitan areas as it is in the countryside.

HISTORICAL ROOTS OF CATALAN REGIONALISM

To understand fully the current manifestations of Catalan regionalism it is essential to go back in time well beyond the Second Republic (1931–39) and even beyond the appearance of modern regional nationalism in the nineteenth century. The roots of current problems go all the way back to the initial formation of the Spanish state in the late fifteenth and early sixteenth centuries.

The marriage of Ferdinand of Aragon and Isabel of Castile led to the formation in the last quarter of the fifteenth century of a joint Spanish monarchy. Ferdinand, who governed Castile as regent after his wife's death in 1504 until his own death in 1516, considered Spain a pluralistic monarchy and respected local rights, laws, privileges, and customs, especially in his patrimonial states, including Catalonia.

Charles I—grandson of Ferdinand and Isabel—and known as Charles V in his capacity as Holy Roman Emperor—inherited the entire Spanish patrimony, ruling it as one country, but its component parts continued to enjoy substantial autonomy. Within this Spanish empire Castile exercised special influence because of her territory and population and because during the formative period of the empire, Castile enjoyed an economic boom, whereas Catalonia was still recovering from the revolutionary upheaval of the previous century. Castile's advantage was further heightened by the shift in the axis of commerce from the Mediterranean to the Atlantic and by her monopoly on trade with the Americas. Finally, the kings of the sixteenth century tended to focus their attention on Castile since they encountered fewer legal barriers to their activities there than in Catalonia and the rest of the former kingdom of Aragon.

As a consequence of these factors, Catalonia, which had been the major component of the Catalan-Aragonese monarchy, lost political importance and influence although it retained control over its own affairs. It did not share the glory or the economic benefits that Castile derived from the Americas, but neither was it required to pay taxes nor supply men to support the armies with which Charles I and Philip II attempted to carry out their policies on the European continent and overseas. Catalan continued to be the language of everyday life, but Castilian displaced it as a literary language.

In the seventeenth century growing demands for men and money with which to bolster Spain's flagging position in Europe led to an attempt by the Crown to bring Catalonia and the other autonomous territories into line with Castile as regards taxes and military service, and generally to tighten up and unify the administration of royal possessions along Castilian patterns. This gave rise to a series of revolts in the course of which the Portuguese succeeded in reestablishing their independence. Catalonia did not escape altogether from Castilian influence, but she did win formal recognition in 1653 of her special liberties which survived unchallenged during the next half century.

A change of dynasty in the early eighteenth century brought with it a sharp change in the status of Catalonia. Philip V, the first of the Bourbon monarchs of Spain, was at first open to Catalan regionalism and allowed the Cortes to confirm the rights (*fueros*) of Catalonia. The opposition of some Catalans to the installation of the Bourbon dynasty together with social and economic unrest, however, had led Catalonia to support the claims of the Austrian pretender to the Spanish throne. His defeat by Philip V signaled the end of Catalonia's autonomous status within the Spanish monarchy. The new monarchy's political and administrative measures applied Castilian laws and institutions to Catalonia and most of the rest of Spain, the result being that these areas for the first time in history were integrated into a unified Spanish political system. Castilian displaced Catalan as the language of government as well as of culture.

Catalonia's loss of political autonomy was offset by her growing economic vitality. The opening up of new markets provided a strong stimulus to Catalan agriculture, manufacturing, and commerce. Population grew rapidly, and by 1760 Catalonia was more prosperous than Castile. The pattern established at this time of an economically strong but politically weak periphery, and a politically strong but economically weak center, has survived to the present with only a few brief parentheses.

The second half of the eighteenth century witnessed the emergence of a Hispanic nationalism which took root throughout Spain, including Catalonia. Regional differences continued to exist, but the Catalans loyally supported the Spanish monarchy, to which they were bound by both economic and affective ties. During the great crisis occasioned by the French Revolution and the Napoleonic wars, the Catalans proved their loyalty and dedication to the Spanish monarchy. A workable equilibrium had been reached in which Catalonia could participate in a larger Spanish national undertaking without renouncing altogether its linguistic and ethnic identity.

Beginning in the 1830s, three factors disturbed this equilibrium and planted the seeds of modern Catalan regional nationalism. Liberals came to power in Spain in the 1830s, and dominated politics for the rest of the century. Most took their inspiration from the political and administrative centralization of Napoleonic France. They imposed on Spain a more centralized government system than it had ever known.

Economic differentiation between a rapidly industrializing Catalonia and a still largely agricultural central and southern Spain grew more pronounced with time. Catalan industry, sheltered behind high tariff walls, geared its production to the Spanish market, but its interests, needs, and outlook were quite different from those of most other regions of Spain. The government at Madrid was reasonably efficient by the standards of underdeveloped Spain, but seriously deficient when viewed from an industrializing Catalonia.

European romanticism and cultural nationalism gave rise in Catalonia to the *renaixença,* or Catalan Renaissance, an attempt by a small group of poets and writers to revive Catalan and make it once again a literary as well as a popular language. The central government's sponsorship of public education in Castilian after 1850 ran directly counter to this effort.

During the last two decades of the nineteenth century, Catalan particularism began to take on political form. It acquired significant political power after Spain's loss of Cuba in 1898. Catalan manufacturers lost important protected markets in Cuba and threw their weight in favor of Catalan regionalist demands for greater autonomy.

From 1906 to 1923 the *Lliga regionalista* dominated Catalan politics. This party, which developed a modern organization and worked to mobilize mass support, was allied to conservative groups in Spanish national politics. Its most concrete success was winning from Madrid in 1913 an administrative arrangement, the *Mancomunitat,* which allowed the four Catalan provinces to act as a unit in matters of local administration, although the new organisms's powers were severely restricted.

The coming of the Primo de Rivera dictatorship in 1923 temporarily put an end to governmental concessions to Catalan regionalism. De Rivera allowed Catalan cultural activities to expand, but dissolved the *Mancomunitat,* thereby fomenting middle-class Catalan aversion to the Spanish state. During the years of the dictatorship, Catalan nationalism remained largely middle-class in its support, but gradually shifted from a right-looking to a left-looking movement. By the end of the dictatorship the left faction, *Acció Catalana,* had become a major force in regional politics.

Catalan regionalists played a leading role in the events which led to the overthrow of the Spanish monarchy and the establishment of the Second Republic in 1931. Since the supporters of the Republic favored decentralization, Catalonia was granted in September 1932 a "Statute of Autonomy" recognizing its position as an "autonomous region within the Spanish state." The statute provided for a Catalan regional government, known as the *Generalitat,* made up of a parliament, an executive council, and a president elected by the parliament. Catalan became "co-official" with Castilian within the borders of Catalonia. The *Generalitat* had the authority to create schools and the University of Barcelona was authorized to provide instruction in Catalan as well as in Castilian. The

Generalitat controlled local government, social services, police and interior order, civil legislation, and the naming of judges.

In the last elections held under the Second Republic, six months before the outbreak of the war, the right-wing Catalan *Lliga* joined the National Front, but the Popular Front (supported by the Catalan left) won by a wide margin in Catalonia. During the war Catalonia was one of the major strongholds of the Republic. Its factories supplied the Republican armies, and Catalan troops, though sometimes reluctant to leave their own region, contributed significantly to the struggle against Franco.

Franco's victory in the Civil War led to the destruction of all local autonomy in Spain, except in the province of Navarre which had supported him enthusiastically during the war. Catalonia was treated as a conquered territory. Like all other parts of Spain, it was governed from Madrid. Catalan disappeared not only from the offices of the government but also from the schools and other areas of public life. Publications and even sermons in Catalan were prohibited, and during the 1940s speaking Catalan on the streets of Barcelona could lead to insult and possible injury.

As the Franco regime attempted to shed some of its more obvious authoritarian aspects in the 1950s and 1960s, it gradually relaxed its restrictions on the use of Catalan. Books and periodicals could appear once again, and an impressive flood of literary and scholarly work in Catalan began to flow. Eventually, schools were allowed to teach the language, but Castilian remained the language of instruction for all other subjects, and the region continued to be governed from Madrid without any concession to Catalan aspirations for control of their own affairs.

Throughout Catalonia, but especially in the highly industrialized province of Barcelona, Catalan regionalist politics merged with other expressions of anti-Franco sentiment. In the final years of Franco's dictatorship, a broad Catalan coalition was built on the basis of regional aspirations and opposition to Franco. Common enmity toward Franco served to unite Catalan groups whose social base, aims, and politics were highly divergent.

THE BASQUE COUNTRY

The Basque country includes four Spanish provinces: Alava, Guipúzcoa, Navarre, and Vizcaya. (See Map 2.2.) Their degree of identification with the Basque cause varies widely and has done so historically. Their combined population of 1.2 million occupies an area of 18,000 km². Vizcaya and Guipúzcoa are densely populated, but the largest city in the region, Bilbao, with 472,000 inhabitants, cannot rival Barcelona (Table 2.4).

MAP 2.2

Map of the Basque Country

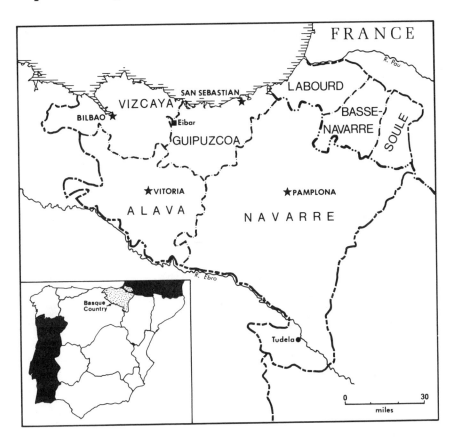

Source: Confederación española de Cajas de Ahorros, *España. Atlas e Indices de sus Terminos municipales* (Madrid, la Confederación, 1969), and Philippe Veynin, *Les Basques* (n.p.: Arthaud, 1947), map out of text.

The more extreme Basque nationalist groups include in their plan for a future Basque state the three historic French regions of Labourd, Basse-Navarre, and Soule. A few Basque activists come from the French side of the Pyrenees, and Spanish Basques have often found temporary refuge there. Basque nationalism is not, however, a powerful factor in the three French provinces and their population does not enter significantly into the dynamics of Spanish Basque politics.

The Basque country is even wealthier than Catalonia. Vizcaya enjoyed in 1971 the highest per capita income of any Spanish province, and

TABLE 2.4

The Basque Country—Estimated Population and Population Density, 1975

Province	Population	Area in Km²	Population per Km²
Alava	240,513	3,047	79
Guipúzcoa	707,308	1,997	354
Navarre	491,076	10,421	47
Vizcaya	1,194,612	2,217	539
Total	2,633,509	17,682	149*

*Average population per km².
Source: INE, *España 1977, Anuario Estadístico* (Madrid, INE, 1977), pp. 10 and 455.

the next two positions were occupied by Guipúzcoa and Alava. The poorest of the Basque provinces, Navarre, ranked in the top one-sixth of the nation and was almost 20 percent above the national average. Taken together the four provinces accounted for 10 percent of Spain's GNP in 1971 (Table 2.5).

As in Catalonia, the demand for labor has produced a strong current of immigration from poorer regions of Spain into the Basque country during most of this century. As early as 1950, slightly over one-fourth of the population of the province of Vizcaya was made up of people born in other provinces. The economic growth of the 1960s increased the influx of immigrants from other regions of Spain. As a result, the percentage of native Basques and of Basque speakers has declined steadily (Table 2.6). Immigrants in the Basque country have been much less successfully assimilated than in Catalonia.

Affective identification with the region is not as widespread in the Basque country as in Catalonia. In 1975 only 32.4 percent of those interviewed said they considered themselves primarily as Basques, whereas 41.1 percent reported that their primary identification was with Spain, and a surprising 19.6 percent considered themselves "citizens of the world." Unlike Catalan nationalism, Basque nationalism has traditionally been much stronger in rural areas than in the cities. A 1969 survey in three of the four Basque provinces found that in rural areas twice as many respondents as in urban areas identified themselves as Basque. The development in recent years of left and extreme left Basque nationalist movements has somewhat changed this situation, but no precise data are available.

The linguistic base of Basque nationalism is weaker than that of Catalan nationalism. Only 19 percent of the people surveyed in the four Basque provinces in 1975 reported that they were able to speak Basque easily. Only half of this group used it most of the time at home, and only 20 percent used it most of the time in other situations. Recently Basque academies have grown in number and popularity and Basque may soon be widely taught in the state schools. Attachment to the Basque language

TABLE 2.5

The Basque Country—Per Capita Income in 1971 and Rank among 50 Spanish Provinces

Province	Per Capita Income in Pesetas	Index (Spanish National Average = 100)	Rank 1971
Alava	101,718	143.75	3
Guipúzcoa	104,111	147.13	2
Navarre	84,160	118.93	8
Vizcaya	105,947	149.72	1

Source: Tamames, *Introducción a la economía española*, 9th ed. (Madrid, Alianza Editorial, 1974), pp. 422–23.

TABLE 2.6

The Basque Country—Immigration*

Province	Number of Persons	Percent of Population of More than Ten Years of Age
Alava	25,873	16
Guipúzcoa	68,075	14
Navarre	34,765	9
Vizcaya	124,325	15
Basque Provinces	251,038	13

*Population of more than ten years of age registered in the province in the 1970 census who were registered in a province of a different region in the 1960 census.

Source: Calculated from *Estudios sociológicos sobre la situación social de España 1975* (Madrid, Editorial Euramérica, 1976), Table VII.5, pp. 74–79.

is cultural, sentimental, and symbolic rather than practical or economic. Hardly any inhabitant of the Basque country is helped in his career by his ability to speak Basque.

HISTORICAL ROOTS OF BASQUE REGIONALISM

Like its Catalan counterpart, Basque nationalism has deep historical roots, and the historical trajectory of Basque regional nationalism is in broad outlines similar to the one we have just traced for Catalan nationalism. At the time of the formation of the Spanish state in the sixteenth century, the provinces of Alava, Guipúzcoa, and Vizcaya had belonged to the crown of Castile for several centuries. The sub-Pyrenean section of Navarre was annexed by Ferdinand in 1512.

The four Basque provinces retained their local customs, institutions, and languages throughout the sixteenth, seventeenth, and eighteenth centuries. Philip V's centralizing measures did not affect them as they did Catalonia. Local questions continued to be decided locally, and taxes were negotiated with the central government and apportioned and collected by provincial assemblies. Since the early middle ages Basque had been limited to domestic usage; Castilian was the language of both government and culture. Basques participated actively in the life of Spain and in all its major enterprises. There was no significant Basque revolt against the Spanish Crown during the *ancien regime*. Though linked by geographic proximity and a common language, the four Basque provinces had no common institutions nor sense of common identity.

The first major challenge to Basque autonomy came from liberal centralism in the 1830s. Basque peasants formed the backbone of Carlist resistance to liberalism. Among the issues of the First Carlist War (1833–39), local liberties, or *fueros*, occupied a central position in the Basque country. At the end of the war, a negotiated settlement was reached which respected the basic *fueros* in matters of administration and taxation. Administrative autonomy was lost definitively only after the Second Carlist War (1870–75). The settlement still allowed Basques to negotiate their taxes with the central government and apportion and collect them locally.

By the end of the nineteenth century, the Basque country, especially Vizcaya, had become a center of Spanish heavy industry and mining. Spanish tariffs worked to the advantage of industries which could not compete with foreign producers. Basque entrepreneurs proved far more daring and modern than their Catalan counterparts, and they participated more actively in the economic and political life of the nation as a whole.

The Basque country could offer no parallel to the Catalan *renaixença*. Throughout the nineteenth century the use of Basque even as a domestic language declined. Several of the greatest literary figures of the early twentieth century—Unamuno and Pio Baroja—were Basques, but they wrote exclusively in Castilian.

Sabino de Arana y Goiri laid the foundations for political Basque nationalism in the 1880s and 1890s. Arana's Basque nationalism was based on close identification with the Church and on a desire to maintain the ethnic purity of the Basque people. The movement gave rise to the Basque Nationalist Party (PNV) that elected its first candidate in 1898 and is still an important exponent of Basque nationalism.

This early Basque nationalism was a very small movement, far less influential than was the Catalan *Lliga*. National Spanish parties of the right and left were more important than the PNV in the politics of the Basque country until the proclamation of the Republic. The relatively small size of the region, the weakness of the linguistic base, the integration of Basque elites into national economic and political life, and the continuing strength of Carlism prohibited the PNV from recruiting mass support prior to the proclamation of the Republic.

Under the Republic Basque nationalism, unlike its Catalan counterpart, remained conservative and Catholic in orientation. The outbreak of the Civil War posed a serious dilemma to Basque nationalists. Their aspirations for regional autonomy dictated that they support the Republic, but their Catholicism and their political and social conservatism made them natural allies of the Nationalist insurgents. In the end, regionalist sentiment prevailed in Guipúzcoa and Vizcaya, which supported the Republic, while Navarre was a stronghold of the Nationalists.

The Franco regime attempted to uproot the remnants of nationalism in the Basque country. In 1937 it deprived the Basque provinces, except Navarre, of economic and administrative autonomy. Repression of the language was less traumatic than in Catalonia, but prohibition of the singing of Basque songs and of the use of Basque symbols provoked clashes between the Civil Guard and the inhabitants of the area.

Unlike the Catalan elite, the members of the Basque elite continued to play important roles in national life during the Franco regime. In the economic sphere this was the natural result of the scope of Basque industrial and financial activities, but Basques were also active in political life. Of the 89 ministers who served in Franco's cabinets between 1938 and 1969, six were from Navarre and six more from other Basque provinces. The men who served in Franco's cabinets had no ties with Basque nationalism. Over half of them were Carlists, and all were closely identified with Franco and his politics. Still, almost twice as many ministers came from the Basque country as from Catalonia, despite the latter region's much larger population. The percentage of ministers from the Basque country was almost two and one-half times as great as the percentage of Basques among the population. The percentage of ministers from Catalonia was only two-thirds the percentage of Catalans in the population.

CHARACTERISTICS OF CATALAN AND BASQUE REGIONALISM

In both Catalonia and the Basque country current demands for regional autonomy are frequently expressed in historical terms. A sense of unjust deprivation of historic rights contributes heavily to the strength of regionalist demands. Available data are not sufficient to permit weighting the various factors which support Basque and Catalan regionalism, but one might surmise that historic tradition is at least as important as any other single item. A historic sense of identity has been kept alive and reinforced in recent decades by reaction against the political center's brutal attempts to crush it. The strength of post-Franco regional nationalism in Catalonia and the Basque country is not due to the "appearance in the last ten years of ethnic nationalism" nor even to "the new political relevance of ethnic loyalties" but rather to a loosening of the restraints that prohibited the manifestation of regional differences under the Franco regime.

Purely ethnic or "racial" factors are not very important in either Catalan or Basque nationalism, although they are more significant in the latter. Linguistic and cultural identity is, as we pointed out, more important in Catalonia than in the Basque country. The identification of most strata of the elite with Catalan culture, or at least language, increases its importance even beyond what a merely quantitative appraisal of its use would suggest. Virtually all Catalan speakers, however, also speak Castilian, and only a small minority wish to see Catalan completely displace Castilian in public life. Under these circumstances, Catalan will acquire an increasingly important role in public life and a growing amount of Catalan programming will appear on radio and television, but Castilian will continue to be widely used in public documents and the mass media.

In other countries, and in other parts of Spain, regional nationalism is to a large extent a result of relative economic deprivation. Clearly this is not the case here. Not only have Catalonia and the Basque country been historically the wealthiest areas of Spain, but they both shared fully in the recent Spanish economic boom. In the period 1947–71, the income of two of the Catalan provinces, Lérida and Gerona, grew significantly less rapidly than the national average, but Barcelona grew somewhat faster than the national rate, and Tarragona was very close to it. Vizcaya, Guipúzcoa, and Navarre also grew at approximately the same rapid rate as the rest of the country, whereas Alava grew almost half again as quickly. Overall, both regions registered a slight increase in their percentage share of GNP.

Both regions carry on a lively commerce with the rest of Spain. Other Spanish regions constitute the best market for Catalan and Basque manufactured products—textiles, steel, fabricated metal goods, and appliances. They also supply the immigrants who do much of the labor. In addition, Bilbao's great banks carry on operations at a national level and have major investments in all parts of Spain. The leaders of the business communities in both regions recognize that they benefit economically from the availability of Spanish markets and of Spanish labor.

Catalan and Basque nationalists complain that they pay dearly for the advantages they derive from being part of Spain. In 1968 Catalonia paid 31 percent of all taxes collected in Spain, whereas only 13 percent of governmental expenditures benefited the region. For the Basque country, the figures were 14 percent and 6 percent. The central government argues that higher tax rates are justified by the regions' economic prosperity and contribute to a socially beneficial transfer of resources from wealthy to poorer regions. Most Catalans and Basques are willing to concede that they ought to pay somewhat higher taxes than other regions, but nationalist sentiment is fostered by the belief that current disparities are excessive.

Demands for autonomy feed on a sense of superior economic skill in comparison with Castile, which exercises administrative and political power but lags behind economically. A disproportion between political and economic power caused by the relative economic weakness of the political center contributes to the discontent of the periphery which feels, with considerable justification, that its interests would be better served by a more decentralized system in which decisions affecting the region could be taken at the regional level.

Except for a small group of Basques, regional nationalists in Spain have not historically called into question the existence of a larger Spanish unity. This Hispanic unity represents not merely a state whose laws they must obey, but a nation whose interests are their own. During the Napoleonic period they fought for Spain. In the twentieth century, they have contested the supremacy of Castile and the way it has run the country's affairs, but they have not severed their emotional ties with Spain. Their plans have frequently been presented as alternate, more efficient, ways of solving the problems of Spain, not merely those of their regions. Cambó, the outstanding Catalan politician of the period prior to the Civil War, worked both for the autonomy of Catalonia and the greatness of Spain. Spain's most distinguished twentieth-century historian, Jaime Vicens Vives, himself a Catalan, wrote:

> Catalanism did not reject Spain as a historic reality. It did reject the way Spain's history had been interpreted by Liberal centralism, the adjustment of the nation's pace to the rhythm of Castile, and the political and economic consequences that these developments entailed. Thus, although Catalanism was the expression of a mentality and language different from that of Castile, it was not therefore necessarily less Hispanic.

3

FROM FRANCO'S DEATH
TO THE REFERENDUM

THE FIRST GOVERNMENT OF THE MONARCHY

After a five-week illness, Francisco Franco died on November 20, 1975. Two days later, Prince Juan Carlos de Borbón was sworn in as king of Spain. The young king is the grandson of Spain's last reigning monarch, Alfonso XIII, who lost his throne upon the proclamation of the Spanish Republic in 1931. King Juan Carlos was a creation of the recently deceased dictator. His claim to the throne was based not on hereditary legitimacy, by whose rules his father, Don Juan, ought to have been king, but on Franco's designation. His education had been carried out under the Caudillo's direction, and he had sworn loyalty to the principles of Franco's National Movement.

The new king was an unknown quantity. Although he had made many public appearances, he had not been free to make public statements on political matters as long as Franco lived. He had been educated by tutors and in the academies of Spain's three armed forces. Many of his closest friends were young military officers with whom he had gone to school. He had traveled extensively, and was thought to harbor sympathy for democratic institutions, but no one knew exactly what policies he would follow. Many observers thought the young king, who had sailed for Spain in the Olympics, showed more athletic than intellectual ability, and few felt that he held great promise as a head of state.

In his first speech to the Cortes, on November 22, Juan Carlos promised to work for a "free and modern society." At the same time, he went out of his way to assure the armed forces of efforts to guarantee their efficiency and strength and expressed confidence that he would have their loyalty. The general pardon announced by the government to mark his accession as king was limited in scope and excluded from its benefits all persons who had been found guilty of or charged with terrorism. This meant that many political prisoners could not benefit from the decree, which the Spanish left severely criticized.

Juan Carlos had several important appointments to make in the early days of his reign. Alejandro Rodríguez de Valcárcel was reaching the end of his seven-year term as President of the Cortes and of the Council of the Realm. If Juan Carlos wanted Spain to be democratized from above, the members of the Cortes would have to be induced to accept reform measures that would amount to their political suicide. The President of the Cortes could either facilitate or hinder that operation. The seventeen-member Council of the Realm was charged with preparing lists of names from which the head of state would choose the President of the Government. It was one of the most hard-line conservative bodies in the country and could be expected to resist attempts to name a more liberal President of the Government. Only a very able and loyal President of the Council could hope to win for the King the freedom of maneuver he needed in this key area.

For these influential positions Juan Carlos chose Torcuato Fernández Miranda, a 60-year-old professor of public law at the University of Madrid and a former Minister as well as Secretary General of the Movement and Vice President of the Government under Carrero Blanco. Fernández Miranda had tutored Juan Carlos in political philosophy. Since then the king had remained close to his former tutor and reportedly felt complete personal confidence in him.

Fernández Miranda was clearly a conservative and a man of the regime. His nomination was intended in part to reassure nervous elements of the Spanish ultra-right. It was a severe disappointment to the partisans of change and reform, who saw in the new President of the Cortes and of the Council of the Realm a serious obstacle to their plans. In retrospect, it is clear that Juan Carlos chose a man of the right to tranquilize the army and the conservatives, but he chose Fernández Miranda primarily as a man on whose personal loyalty he could count fully. He was the king's own man, willing to carry out Juan Carlos's desires independently of his own political preferences. His legal knowledge would prove invaluable when the time came to use his position as President of the Cortes to force that body of Franco appointees to accept a thorough transformation of the regime's institutions.

The disappointment caused by Fernández Miranda's appointment increased greatly when Juan Carlos decided to confirm Carlos Arias Navarro as President of the Government. The 65-year-old lawyer had begun his career as a public prosecutor during the Republic. During the Civil War he served as Nationalist prosecutor in Málaga where the repression was particularly severe. From 1944 to 1957 he was civil governor of various provinces. In 1957 he became Spain's top policeman as Director General of Security under Camilo Alonso Vega, one of the most severe ministers of the interior of the Franco era. After serving as Mayor of Madrid from 1965 to 1973, Arias was named Minister of the Interior by Carrero Blanco. Franco chose him to succeed Carrero after a bomb planted by Basque terrorists took the life of the President of the Government in December 1973.

As President, Arias had implemented a number of mild reforms designed to give Spaniards somewhat more voice in local government and to allow the formation of the political associations discussed in Chapter 1. He had defrauded, however, the high hopes stirred by his speech of February 12, 1974, and his confirmation as first President of the Government of the monarchy on December 5, 1975, represented a serious setback for the partisans of liberalization.

Arias's new government, announced on December 12, contained only three holdovers from the previous cabinet among its twenty members. Prominent positions went to two of the leading *aperturistas*: Manual Fraga Irribarne, as Minister of the Interior, and José María Areilza, as Foreign Minister. The changes in personnel gave the new government a somewhat more liberal image. It was more sincerely dedicated to reform than its predecessor, but was still very closely identified with the continuance of the Franco regime. All of its members had served Franco in one capacity or another, and the government differed more in tone than in substance from its immediate predecessors. Its record over the course of its seven-month existence would confirm the initial impression that it would pursue reform but only in a very cautious and hesitant fashion.

The limited character of the pardon granted on the occasion of Juan Carlos's proclamation seemed to signify that Franco's death would not lead to the reconciliation which many Spaniards felt was the key to any profound and lasting solution to the problems inherited by the post-Franco era. The long-awaited passing of the dictator aroused hopes and expectations which at first seemed destined to be frustrated. An opposition that had waited for years for this moment demanded rapid sweeping change, but the Arias government responded to its demands in ways not very different from those of Franco's governments. It prohibited Socialists from holding a press conference, used massive detachments of police to break up demonstrations in Madrid, and arrested leaders of the moderate left for illegal assembly. A deteriorating economic situation increased the tension. In January 1976, the government decreed a wage freeze. Workers responded with strikes. Workers demanding higher wages struck the Madrid subway, the post office, and the railroads. The government responded by using troops to run the subway and by militarizing postal and railway workers.

Arias announced that he would make a major policy speech on January 28, 1976 to explain his program of political reform. For weeks, Madrid was alive with discussion of the forthcoming speech, but the program Arias presented to the Cortes on the 28th disappointed even the most moderate reformers by its vague and inconclusive character and by its failure to put forward a concrete plan and a definite timetable. The cover of Spain's most widely read weekly news magazine, *Cambio 16*, described it as "Arias's screeching halt" and a leading business magazine called it "a step backwards."

The draconian decree-law on terrorism promulgated on August 27, 1975, was modified in early February 1976, but not abrogated. Its mandatory death penalty for terrorism was abolished and the defense given somewhat greater rights, but house searches without court orders were still permitted and offenses committed by members of miltiary or paramilitary organizations such as ETA V remained subject to military jurisdiction.

During the month of February massive demonstrations in favor of amnesty and regional autonomy took place in Barcelona. Although prohibited by the police, and broken up with considerable violence, they did not claim any victims. The first major bloodshed took place in March in Vitoria, in the Basque province of Alava. During a "day of struggle" in support of striking workers, five demonstrators were killed by the police and some one hundred persons were injured. The incident provoked great tension, both in the Basque country and throughout Spain. Strikes and demonstrations broke out all over Spain and virtually paralyzed the Basque country.

During the first four months of the monarchy, expectations of greater freedom, demands for regional autonomy in Catalonia and the Basque country, and economic grievances of workers suffering from the effects of a deteriorating economic situation clashed with the government's determination to permit only gradual, orderly change. The result was a wave of demonstrations, strikes, terrorist activity, and police violence, which seemed to threaten the country's stability and to forebode either revolution or military intervention. Nonetheless, the government did not lose control of the situation and continued on its slow, cautious path toward reform, proposing in February and March legislation that would widen the right of assembly and political association.

In March 1976, the two major coalitions of opposition groups—*Junta democrática* and *Plataforma de convergencia democrática*—came together to form a single opposition front, officially known as Democratic Coordination, and popularly referred to as the *Platajunta*.

During Arias's second ministry, opposition groups continued to be illegal, but the press reported regularly on the declarations of the *Coordinación democrática* and of other opposition forces. The government's attitude varied sharply from day to day and week to week. Opposition leaders who had expressed their opinions freely one day might find themselves in jail a few weeks later for seemingly less offensive statements, but in most cases they were not held long. Public meetings and demonstrations sometimes took place without incident, but at other times they caused violent clashes with the police. The common thread running through this confused picture was a growing legitimacy of the opposition, which gradually won for itself a place as an accepted actor on the political scene. Even the Spanish Communist Party, which suffered the brunt of the repression, managed to make itself heard with increasing frequency in the legal press and to give public proof of its existence by organizing strikes and demonstrations.

The opposition spoke stridently about a "democratic clean break," but in fact showed considerable patience and seemed to recognize that it might be necessary to adopt a slower pace than desired so as not to endanger eventual success. This moderation of the opposition, its ability to keep up pressure in favor of change without going so far as to provoke a violent reaction by the right, was one of the keys to the political situation throughout the entire second Arias government and would continue to be of great importance in the future.

ARIAS'S REFORM

On April 28, Prime Minister Arias finally presented to the Cortes a program of political reforms, and a timetable calling for a referendum in October 1976 and general elections in the first semester of 1977. Arias's plan called for all reforms to be instituted by the government and approved by the Cortes before being proposed to the country at large in the referendum. The Prime Minister insisted that all changes must come from above and explicitly rejected the opposition's repeated appeals for a constituent assembly. "There is no room in our political universe," he said, "for any revolutionary idea of a sharp break [with the past] nor for any petition for opening a constituent period."

This statement, even more than the details of the measures Arias proposed, revealed the limitations of reform carried out by the elitist and authoritarian "reformers" who made up the government. Arias's proposals excluded all direct input of the public or the opposition into the process of reform. The continuity between the Arias government and Franco was clearly marked by their common assumption that the government formulates policy, the opposition criticizes (more freely under Arias), but cannot change it, and the citizens simply wait to see what will happen.

The first of the reform measures to be approved was the legalization of political meetings. On May 25, the Cortes voted by a wide margin to permit all political groups except Communists to meet in nonpublic places without need for government approval as long as they gave a 72-hour advance notice of their intention. Street demonstrations, however, could be held only with government permission, which would have to be requested at least ten days in advance.

The legislation did not specify under what conditions permission for street demonstrations would be granted, and its application proved arbitrary. Local authorities were much more strict in some provinces than in others, so that petitions to hold very similar types of meetings were accepted in one city and turned down in another. The amount of discretionary power left to the government was indicative of the Arias government's attitude toward change and its desire to retain as much control as possible. Nonetheless, the new legislation did represent a major step forward.

The ease with which the legislation authorizing political meetings was approved by the Cortes seemed to indicate that body would not seriously obstruct the government's reform program, but the next step, the legalization of political parties, met with more resistance. During two days of acrimonious debate, the right castigated the proposal as a direct attack on Franco's legacy and as opening the door to Marxism. Shortly before the final vote, Adolfo Suárez, then the minister in charge of the National Movement, argued strongly in favor of its passage, going so far as to describe it as a way of "completing the work" of Franco. "The government," he said, "which is the legitimate manager of this historic moment, has the responsibility of setting in motion the necessary mechanisms for the definitive consolidation of a modern democracy. To achieve this, the starting point lies in the recognition of a pluralistic society." In a roll-call vote on June 9, 1976, 338 members voted in favor, 91 against, 24 abstained, and 108 were absent.

Under the new legislation, a group seeking legal recognition as a party had to present a request to the Minister of the Interior for inscription in a special register. The government then had two months in which to accept or reject the request. If it was rejected, an appeal could be made to the Supreme Court, which was also empowered to suspend or dissolve a party at the government's request.

The new legislation required changes in Spain's penal code, which defined forming or belonging to a political party as a criminal offense. Approval of these changes appeared to most observers a foregone conclusion after the passage of the law itself. The Cortes, however, refused to proceed immediately and requested that the text be sent back to committee. The government could probably have won on another immediate roll-call vote, but chose to accept the delay rather than force a showdown.

As it turned out, approval of the changes in the penal code would not be forthcoming until July 14, by which time Arias had been replaced by Suárez.

The fall of the Arias government prevented discussion and implementation of the rest of the reforms he had proposed, but it is worthwhile to review them in order to form a more exact idea of the kind of transition he envisioned and of its limitations.

The Arias government's proposals for reforming the Cortes called for a bicameral legislature. The lower house of 300 members would have been elected by universal suffrage. The upper chamber would have been a complex organism. Two hundred members would have been elected on the basis of universal suffrage (four for each of Spain's 50 provinces). The king would have appointed 25 senators and another 25 would have been chosen by provincial and local councils and by professional groups such as the associations of Spanish doctors, engineers, lawyers, etc. The 40 current members of the National Council of the Movement, appointed by General Franco, would have become lifetime members of the Senate. The eventual outcome of this proposal would have depended on the powers of the two houses, which the Arias government did not specify, and on the composition of the provincial and local councils, unions, and business organizations, whose reorganization and restructuring were still pending when the Arias government fell.

Arias's program called for revising but not abolishing the Council of the Realm. The future powers of the revised Council of the Realm were not spelled out in the new proposal, but it appears that Arias intended it to continue to have the right to propose three names from which the king would choose his prime minister.

The Arias government had also promised on May 7 to introduce legislation which would have allowed workers and employers freely to form professional associations. This was the first time since the Civil War that a Spanish government had declared its intention to allow free labor unions outside the framework of the state-controlled syndicates, but no indication was given as to the exact nature of the proposed legislation nor as to the fate of the existing *sindicatos* organization.

The interest of the press and of Madrid's political leaders was focused throughout the lifetime of the Arias government on questions of political reform. The economic situation had deteriorated in an atmosphere of drift. Public opinion polls showed that most people were concerned about unemployment and inflation, while only a small minority ranked the uncertain political future as their greatest concern. Yet the government seemed entirely absorbed in politics, and its Finance Minister, Juan Miguel Villar Mir, was regarded by many as its weakest and most inept member.

The business and financial community was extremely critical of the Arias government, which it accused of lacking any coherent economic policy and allowing the nation to slide toward economic disaster. The only major measure taken by the government, the unexpected ten-percent devaluation of the peseta in February 1976, was not accompanied by the complementary steps which would have been necessary to make it effective and it became in fact one of the sources of inflationary pressure.

The limited character of Spain's arsenal of economic instruments further complicated the situation. The fiscal system was rigid and inefficient, and offered very few possible avenues for increasing revenues. Expenditures could, of course, be decreased, but even in this field the system offered little flexibility. Current government expenditures on goods and services amounted to only 9.5 percent of GNP, the lowest percentage of any OECD member and less than two-thirds of the average of OECD member countries. The Arias government spoke of fiscal reform, but made no substantial progress toward implementing it. It could, of course, plead shortness of time; but the fact is that it failed not only to take energetic short-term corrective measures, but also to make a serious effort to reform or create basic instruments of economic policy implementation. From an economic point of view, the Arias government must be classified as a failure, no matter what standard of judgment is adopted.

From a political viewpoint, it represented an attempt to take those measures of liberalization and democratization which were required by internal pressures and by the international situation, while retaining as large a measure of discretionary control for the government as possible, and at the same time preserving as much of the institutions of the Franco regime as possible. Arias attempted in Spain what Marcello Caetano attempted in Portugal: to maintain the fundamental structure of the regime after the death of the dictator, while making those changes that seemed essential for him to stay in power. Although it was not immediately apparent at the time, his fall in July 1976 represented the end of that attempt. In the following period the struggle would be between proponents of more thoroughgoing reform from within and above, without any sharp break in continuity, and proponents of a clean break with the past in the name of entirely new democratic institutions to be created from below.

Two factors moved Juan Carlos to request Arias's resignation in July 1976: his inability or unwillingness to proceed fast enough to disarm his critics and return some measure of peace and stability to the nation; and his devotion to Franco, rather than to the king. Of these two, the second may well have been the most important. Juan Carlos found in Fernández Miranda a loyal collaborator who placed his wishes above all other considerations. Arias looked for guidance and inspiration not to the young king but to the deceased Caudillo, a large portrait of whom continued to hang in his office, where only a small photograph of Juan Carlos could be seen. In addition, Juan Carlos sensed that the pace of reform under Arias was too slow. The combination of worsening economic conditions and limited, reluctant political reform was leading to growing popular discontent which threatened to undermine the stability of the monarchy itself.

PRESIDENT SUÁREZ

For months prior to Arias's fall, politicians and journalists had been speculating on the name of his probable successor. Almost everyone agreed that it would be either the Foreign Minister, José María de Areilza, Count of Motrico, or the Minister of the Interior, Manuel Fraga Irribarne. Both were willing to push ahead quickly with the political reforms the king wanted. Since Areilza had excellent contacts with the opposition and would thus be able to proceed with less difficulty from strikes and demonstrations, most observers thought he was the most likely candidate.

Juan Carlos, however, was looking for other qualities in his next President of the Government. He wanted someone personally loyal to him, with whom he could work well, and if possible not too much older than himself. In addition, he was determined to avoid a sharp break with the past, continuing to work through the existing institutions, manned almost exclusively by Franco appointees. This meant that it was more important for the future president to have close contacts with the political establishment and to be able to maneuver within its institutions than for him to be on good terms with the left-wing opposition.

It seems highly probable that the king chose Adolfo Suárez González before he asked Arias to resign, and that he instructed Fernández Miranda to see to it that Suárez would be one of the three candidates proposed to him by the Council of the Realm. The nomination took Spain entirely by surprise. The 43-year-old politician had occasionally been mentioned as a rising star on the political horizon, but no one had thought of him as a serious candidate for president.

Born in 1932, the son of a state prosecutor, he studied law in Salamanca and Madrid. Even prior to finishing his studies, he attracted the attention of Fernando Herrero Tejedor, Civil Governor of the province of Avila. Herrero Tejedor gave him a minor administrative post in Avila, and in 1958 brought him with him to the General Secretariat of the National Movement as his private secretary. After occupying a number of bureaucratic posts, Suárez in 1965 became program director of the state-owned television network and shortly thereafter director of its first channel. While working in television, he successfully ran for a seat as a family representative in the Cortes.

From 1968 to 1970 Suárez was Civil Governor of Segovia province, and for the following three years, Director General of Radio and Television. In March 1975, Herrero Tejedor made him Under Secretary of the National Movement. Members of the National Council of the Movement chose him in preference to Franco's son-in-law to fill a vacancy in that stronghold of regime faithfuls, thereby highlighting his prestige among regime politicians. When Herrero Tejedor died in an accident during the summer of 1975, Suárez moved over to a position as the government's representative in the privately owned national telephone company.

Suárez worked actively in the founding of one of the most important "political associations" formed under Arias, the Union of the Spanish People (UDPE). In July 1975, he was elected President of the UDPE and in December he entered the first government of the monarchy as Secretary General of the National Movement. Despite his close ties to the Movement, Suárez was far removed from the "blue shirts" of the Falange. He was a pragmatic politician who had served the Movement to foster his own career, but with no deep commitment to its principles.

As soon as Suárez's nomination was announced, a cry of outrage went up not only from the left-wing opposition, but from the *aperturistas* and their numerous supporters in the press as well. Areilza, Fraga, and three other ministers immediately announced that they would not consider serving in a government headed by Suárez. It was the first time since the Civil War that ministers had publicly stated they would not continue to serve in a new government. The refusal was taken as a clear confirmation that Suárez's nomination meant the end of reform and a victory of the opponents of liberalization. The press, which had acquired considerably more freedom since Franco's death, bitterly attacked the king's choice. A well-known commentator entitled his article in *El Pais*, "What an Error, What an Immense Error!"

The refusal of Areilza and Fraga to continue in office complicated Suárez's task of putting together a new government; however, their stand would eventually work in his favor by giving him more freedom of action and eliminating the necessity of sharing the limelight with others. Most of the leading politicians considered at the time as being liberal wanted nothing to do with Suárez. On the other hand, he did not want to draw on the Falange for his ministers. Instead, he turned for support to a group of right-wing Christian Democrats headed by Alfonso Osorio. Osorio played a key role in the formation of the first Suárez government, of which he would be vice president. Of the ten new ministers, two belonged to his group of "Tacitos" and three more belonged to another right-wing Christian Democrat group, the Spanish Democratic Union (UDE). Three new ministers were members of Suárez's UDPE, and the remaining two belonged to no organized political group.

In most ways, the Suárez government was similar to its predecessor, but it did signal an important generational shift in Spanish politics. Not only were the old men of the Franco regime not represented in its ranks, but Suárez skipped over the better part of the intermediate generation to find his ministers among men who had been university students in the 1950s. The median age of the ten new ministers was 43. Most of them were little known. Not a single one could be considered a leading political figure at the time of his appointment. They had not fought in the Civil War and in most cases had no memories of it. Like most of their contemporaries, the new ministers wanted change and were less obsessed with the idea of violence than the older generation. Most of them had made their careers within the administration of the Franco regime, but they were not ideologically identified with Francoism. King Juan Carlos finally had a government headed by his own man and made up of his contemporaries.

When Suárez took over from Arias, the Spanish economy was suffering from stagnation, inflation, unemployment, and a deteriorating balance of payments. Real GDP had increased only about one percent in 1975. In the first five months of 1976, prices had increased almost 12 percent, including a spectacular 4.6 percent rise in May. According to official figures, unemployment had risen to over five percent. This meant more than 700,000 unemployed, and most economists believed that even these figures seriously understated the actual extent of the problem. There was a growing pool of hard-core unemployed. Almost a quarter of those without work had been without a job for a year or more. Young people entering the labor market were finding it all but impossible to obtain employment. In 1975, imports had exceeded exports by $8.6 billion. The devaluation of the peseta decreed by Arias in February did provide some temporary relief, but the trade deficit would still reach $7.3 billion in 1976.

The new president felt his appointed government lacked the political authority necessary to impose a stern austerity policy and make it stick. The economic measures the government did take were timid and inadequate. In October, the government announced an economic stability plan, calling for price controls on basic commodities and limiting salary increases to the rise in the cost of living, but it provided no mechanisms for enforcing these limits. It also increased income taxes by ten percent and attempted to control energy consumption and imports. In February 1977, a new economic program extended price controls, provided some export incentives, and called for holding the increase of the money supply to 21 percent in order to keep inflation below 17 percent.

These measures may have had some slight beneficial effects, but they did nothing to solve the basic imbalances of the Spanish economy. Through April 1977, prices rose even faster than they had in the corresponding months of 1976, increasing 9.2 percent in four months. The commercial balance deteriorated further, and unemployment showed no improvement. Fundamentally there was, as a business magazine observed, "no strategy, good or bad, to permit the country to face the present pessimistic situation."

Like Arias, Suárez deliberately chose to concentrate his attention on politics. Reading the Spanish press and listening to Spaniards talk about politics in the summer of 1976, one could not help but be impressed by the extent of an ingenuous faith in universal manhood suffrage as a cure-all for the country's ills. Both commitment to democracy and belief in its efficacy in solving the country's political problems were in large part superficial. Spaniards themselves had had little experience with democracy and what experience they had was not felicitous. Economic equality rather than "bourgeois freedom" had long been the rallying cry of the intellectual left, which dominated the universities and was becoming increasingly influential in the press. Nonetheless, for the moment the appeal of democracy was very widespread. Spanish politicians of both the center and the left talked about free elections with almost mystical fervor, reminiscent of early and mid-nineteenth century liberals. It was considered a lack of good taste to suggest that an elected body, whether constituent or legislative, might well find itself faced with intractable problems and prove no more efficient in finding a solution to the country's problems than the appointed administrations of the Franco period.

The new president and the king were determined to give Spain the freer, more democratic institutions most Spaniards wanted. They both rejected, however, the opposition's call for a clean break with the Francoist past through the convening of a constituent assembly, as well as its contention that democracy could not be handed down from above. Suárez opted to continue to work within the framework of the institutions established by Franco: the Cortes, the National Council of the Movement, and the Council of the Realm. The political problem was, then, extremely difficult: to devise a set of institutions sufficiently democratic to satisfy the country's demand for greater freedom and participation; to force the Cortes and other bodies held over from the Franco period to accept them; to keep the armed forces from blocking them; and to convince the opposition, or at least the public at large, that they were genuine enough to participate in.

Suárez set to work immediately to produce some sense of national reconciliation, as a vital prerequisite for his reforms. In his acceptance speech, he studiously avoided all references to the Civil War, to the National Movement, and to the upcoming anniversary of the July 18th military uprising that gave birth to the Franco regime. His appeal for support was directed to all Spaniards, without the distinction between good, law-abiding supporters of the regime and other Spaniards, which had characterized the rhetoric of all his predecessors.

National reconciliation would be merely a matter of words as long as the opponents of the regime continued to be held in prison for political offenses. The month of July witnessed an enormous number of pro-amnesty demonstrations in the Basque country and throughout Spain, organized by numerous democratic opposition groups, including the Democratic Coordination, the Assembly of Catalonia, and the Democratic Assembly of the Basque country. In its first policy statement, the Suárez cabinet promised amnesty to all political prisoners except those convicted of violence against persons. The amnesty, granted on July 31, 1976, affected about half of the slightly over 600 political prisoners then serving sentences or awaiting trial. The rest, mostly Basques convicted of or charged with terrorism or attacks against the police, were excluded from its benefits.

The initial enthusiasm which greeted the announcement of amnesty soon dissipated in the face of the decree's excruciatingly slow application, but the granting of the amnesty did lend some credibility to the government's claim of wanting to close the books on the Civil War. The measure was probably as broadly conceived as was possible at the time. The weak, newly formed Suárez government was in no position to antagonize the police and the army by pardoning terrorists and others involved in attacks on the forces of order.

On July 14, Suárez brought back to the Cortes the modification of the penal code permitting membership in political parties, which the Arias government had failed to get approved. The debate centered chiefly on legalization of the Communist Party. The Cortes rejected a proposal sponsored by the extreme right which would have declared illegal "national and internatinal Communist groups, associations, and parties." It approved the project presented on June 9 which outlawed those associations "subject to international discipline that aim to implant a totalitarian system."

The law approved in June already declared illegal all parties that engaged in violent subversion and those that sought "the destruction of the judicial, political, social, and economic system." This broadly worded provision gave the government wide discretionary powers, more than sufficient to ban not only the Communist Party but the Socialists and possibly even the Social Democrats, if it so desired. Anti-communists wanted, however, to close the door to legalization of the Communist Party at any time in the future. Most opposition parties had made legalization of the PCE a major plank in their platforms, and the PCE itself had worked very hard to convince the public that its legalization was an essential requirement for any democratic government. The government wanted legislation that would leave it as much freedom as possible in the future, and the government won.

During the summer and early fall of 1976, the opposition shifted its attention from amnesty to reform. Strikes and demonstrations kept up the pressure on the government, while opposition politicians attempted to increase their direct influence on the shape of future reform. Through midsummer, the Democratic Coordination called for a sequence of events basically similar to those that had led to the establishment of the Second Republic in 1931. The anti-Franco opposition, united in the Democratic Coordination, would overthrow the prevailing political system through mass action and then form a provisional government with the double objective of establishing a regime of liberty and guaranteeing free elections for a constituent assembly.

The Communist members of the Democratic Coordination were especially anxious to woo the center and right opposition, since their participation in a Communist-sponsored organization would be a major step forward in the PCE's persevering campaign to win recognition for itself as a legitimate political party, entitled to participate fully in the political process. In part for that very reason, Liberals, Social Democrats, and, in general, the center and center-right opposition refused to join the Democratic Coordination, which they viewed as an essentially Communist-Socialist organization whose character was only slightly modified by the presence of a number of left-wing Christian Democrats in its midst. The Democratic Coordination was the most important single opposition group, but it could not claim to speak for the entire opposition.

In late summer the Democratic Coordination stopped calling for all other groups to enter its organization. Rather, it suggested the formation of a new, broader opposition coalition which would include itself, the various regional opposition groups, and the other democratic opposition parties. This coalition would not attempt to overthrow the government through mass action and take its place. It would negotiate the establishment of a new, much more broadly based government which would include representatives of the forces currently in the government as well as of the opposition. This new government, backed by an ample consensus, would then take the steps necessary to open a constituent period.

The growing pressure from the left strengthened Suárez's none-too-strong commitment to democratic reform. In August, he met with at least 13 leaders of the left opposition, including Felipe González, the leader of the Spanish Socialist Workers' Party. Little came of the meetings. Suárez was particularly adamant on the question of the Communist Party, whose legalization the entire left opposition demanded as a condition of its cooperation. The government refused even to grant passports to the Communist leaders Santiago Carrillo and Dolores Ibarruri when they requested permission to enter the country after the Party decided in August to emerge from its clandestine activity and set up sections throughout Spain. Suárez was willing to discuss with the opposition, but not to negotiate, and certainly not to form a new, more broadly based government. He was firmly convinced of the enormous advantage he held by being in power and was determined to carry out the reform on his own initiative.

POLITICAL REFORM

On September 11, Suárez addressed the nation on television, outlining in general terms a project of political reform which would be presented to the Cortes the next day. Time and again, he stressed the idea of popular sovereignty and insisted that only the freely elected Cortes of the future could solve Spain's economic problems and decide the shape of its political future. He explicitly deferred until after free elections both major economic reforms and the question of autonomy for the Basques and Catalans. He admitted that a constituent assembly would be necessary, though he carefully avoided the use of that term.

The poltical reform bill presented to the Cortes the next day called for the establishment of a bicameral legislature. The members of both houses would be elected by direct, secret, universal suffrage, except that the king would be able to appoint one-sixth of the senators. The "organic" representation of the Franco Cortes disappeared in favor of direct election. The Cortes would have power to write a constitution, and the king would be empowered, if he wished, to submit all constitutional measures to a referendum. In addition, he would receive the right to submit to referendum on his own initiative any constitutional or other matters of national interest.

One of the keys to the success or failure of Suárez's reforms would be the attitude of the army. Before presenting his plan to the public, he had met with top military leaders who apparently agreed to support it. In late September he took a major step forward by replacing the conservative General Fernando de Santiago as First Vice President for Defense. Santiago, whom Suárez had inherited from Arias, was bitterly opposed to Suárez's planned reforms, especially the legalization of trade unions other than the official "vertical syndicates." His replacement was General Manuel Gutiérrez Mellado, a close supporter of Juan Carlos and a liberal among high-ranking Spanish officers.

Santiago's forced resignation caused some unrest among other Spanish army leaders, but failed to swing them over into opposition to the king's government. Only one general, former Commander of the Civil Guard Carlos Iniesta Cano, an ultra-Francoist, publicly manifested his solidarity with Santiago, and he was immediately disciplined. Juan Carlos's personal popularity among the military and his prestige as the incarnation of the legitimate authority of the state proved more influential than the generals' aversion to democratic reform. The king's government demonstrated its strength in the face of the most conservative military opinion and won for itself greatly enhanced freedom of maneuver for the future.

The program of political reform faced considerable opposition from the members of the Cortes. Appointed in their vast majority by Franco, they were being asked to give up their positions and to vote out of existence the institution in which they had served. For several seeks it seemed that the right might gather enough strength to vote down Suárez's proposal. In the end, however, under unremitting pressure from the government and the skillful direction of its president, Fernández Miranda, the last Franco Cortes demonstrated its characteristic willingness to approve every proposal submitted by the government. It modified the draft to make a referendum on constitutional matters mandatory rather than optional, but 425 of 497 votes were cast in favor of the law.

The reform measures approved by the Cortes were submitted to a national referendum on December 15, 1976. From the moment Suárez announced it, the opposition had rejected his political reform bill not on the basis of its content, but of its origin. For months the chief demand of the opposition had been that all fundamental reforms be negotiated between the government and the opposition. Suárez had presented a law of transcendental importance without even consulting the opposition, much less negotiating with it. The opposition further feared that if the government continued to act on its own initiative and without any outside checks, it would use its power to manage the announced elections in its own favor.

The extreme right campaigned for a "no" vote, but there was no real doubt that the reforms would be approved. The issue at stake in the referendum was rather the path of future reforms. The question of reform from above versus reform from below that had agitated Spanish political life during the previous year was in a real sense being submitted to a public vote. A "yes" vote would be interpreted as approval not only of the substance of the reform, but of the way it had been carried out. Massive abstention would constitute a rejection of Juan Carlos's and Suárez's type of government-controlled change. Democratic opposition groups were in a difficult situation, however, since no matter how much they resented the way the proposals had been prepared, they heartily approved of their substance. The issue was not an easy one to explain to the public. It was hard to tell voters that they should not approve a system that called for free elections.

Communists, Socialists, regional nationalists, and some Christian Democrats did campaign in favor of abstention, but only halfheartedly.

TABLE 3.1

Results of the Referendum, December 1976

Province	Abstained Percent of Registered Voters	Yes	No Percent of Votes Emitted	Blank and Null Percent of Votes Cast
Alava	13.7	91.9	5.4	2.7
Albacete	17.0	95.5	1.9	2.6
Alicante	14.9	95.3	2.5	2.2
Almeria	18.3	96.9	1.6	1.5
Avila	17.7	96.1	2.1	1.8
Badajoz	18.8	95.9	2.1	2.0
Baleares	17.4	95.1	3.2	1.7
Barcelona	27.7	92.9	4.9	2.2
Burgos	17.2	92.6	4.0	3.4
Cáceres	19.3	96.2	1.9	1.9
Cádiz	19.0	95.6	2.7	1.7
Castellón	11.4	95.9	2.2	1.9
Ciudad Real	16.9	94.8	2.1	3.1
Córdoba	17.4	96.0	2.0	2.0
La Coruña	30.5	95.5	2.7	1.8
Cuenca	14.2	95.0	1.8	3.2
Gerona	18.2	94.4	3.9	1.7
Granada	18.1	96.5	1.8	1.7
Guadalajara	15.9	93.0	2.6	4.4
Guipúzcoa	55.1	91.5	5.8	2.7
Huelva	18.7	96.6	1.3	2.1
Huesca	16.3	95.5	1.4	3.1
Jaén	19.0	96.1	2.5	1.4
León	22.9	94.9	2.1	3.0
Lérida	21.0	95.3	1.5	3.2
Logroño	14.2	95.2	1.7	3.1
Lugo	30.1	94.8	2.0	3.2
Madrid	21.2	92.3	3.9	3.8
Málaga	19.8	95.7	2.0	2.3
Murcia	17.4	95.9	2.3	1.8
Navarre	26.4	92.8	2.9	4.3
Orense	36.4	96.8	1.4	1.8
Oviedo	28.3	92.9	4.1	3.0
Palencia	16.8	93.5	3.3	3.2
Las Palmas	16.6	96.0	1.6	2.4
Pontevedra	28.4	95.2	2.2	2.6

Salamanca	15.7	94.8	1.8	3.4
Santa Cruz de				
Tenerife	32.4	96.4	1.7	1.9
Santander	20.5	89.7	6.6	3.7
Segovia	13.8	94.3	2.4	3.3
Seville	19.5	95.8	1.6	2.6
Soria	17.2	94.5	1.9	3.6
Tarragona	32.1	95.2	1.7	3.1
Teruel	13.5	95.0	2.1	2.9
Toledo	13.4	91.7	6.0	2.3
Valencia	15.1	94.3	2.5	3.2
Valladolid	16.7	91.3	3.8	4.9
Vizcaya	46.8	90.7	3.9	2.5
Zamora	16.7	93.3	2.6	4.1
Zaragoza	15.1	93.8	2.4	3.8
Ceuta	25.5	94.4	3.6	2.0
Melilla	20.8	93.0	4.7	2.3

Source: La Actualidade Española, December 20–26, 1976, p. 13.

The government made massive use of television and billboard ads to increase participation in the referendum. "Don't let anyone else decide for you," the government urged voters from innumerable posters.

The right's campaign failed miserably, obtaining only 2.6 percent "no" votes. Only in four provinces did it reach five percent of the vote. In the first real test of strength, the die-hard Francoists proved far weaker than anyone had imagined. The government obtained a resounding success. The percentage of "yes" votes was 94.2, with three percent blank and 0.2 percent null. Of the eligible voters, 77.7 percent cast a ballot. The 22.3 percent abstentions were heavily concentrated in areas with relatively strong regional nationalist movements. Only seven of the 50 provinces reached 30 percent abstentions. Of these, three were in Galicia, two in the Basque country, one in Catalonia, and one in the Canary Islands. Abstention could be attributed as much to regional sentiment as to rejection of Suárez's method of reform from above (see Table 3.1).

The year 1976 had witnessed a three-sided struggle among *Caetanismo* (Arias), reform from above (Suárez), and a "clean break" with the past leading to reform from below (opposition). The results of the referendum signaled the victory of reform from above, and greatly strengthened the position of both the Suárez government and the monarchy.

4

FROM THE REFERENDUM
TO THE JUNE 1977 ELECTIONS

Suárez had promised that if his reform law was passed, he would hold general elections sometime before the end of the first semester of 1977. For the elections to be held and to represent a meaningful step toward democracy, a number of conditions had to be met: an electoral law had to be prepared and approved; political parties had to be organized and granted legal recognition; the public had to be convinced that it ought to participate in the elections; and the country had to be kept from descending into chaos, a situation which would vitiate the electoral results even if it did not bring the army out into the streets.

The opposition had apparently come to realize, even before the referendum was held, that the most it could hope to do in the near future was to influence government policy through conversations and negotiations between its representatives and the President of the Government. Recognizing that there was no short-term prospect of overthrowing the government or of forcing a reorganization in which members of the opposition would be called to serve as ministers, the opposition formed in early December a ten-member committee to negotiate with Suárez the terms of the parliamentary elections. The committee included one representative for the liberal parties, one for the Social Democrats, one for the Christian Democrats, two for the Socialists, one for the Communists, one for the nongovernment labor movement, and one each for Catalonia, Galicia, and the Basque country.

Virtually the entire opposition agreed to a list of objectives that its representatives should pursue: legal recognition of all political parties and trade unions; recognition, protection, and guarantees of political and trade union freedoms; rapid dissolution of the political apparatus of the

54

National Movement and real political neutrality of the public administration; a true political amnesty; equal access to the state-controlled television and radio; negotiation of the norms for the elections and their democratic control; and recognition of the need to give political form to all the regions that make up the Spanish state.

THE ELECTORAL LAW

The political reform law approved in the December 15 referendum contained only general and vague indications of how the elections should be held. It specified direct, secret, universal manhood suffrage and, for the lower house, "proportional representation, applying corrective measures to avoid excessive fragmentation of the chamber." It set at 350 the total number of seats in the lower house but did not determine how they would be apportioned among Spain's fifty provinces. Since the referendum attributed to the government the right to regulate the elections, there was no need to go back to the Cortes. The details were worked out in consultation between Suárez and representatives of the opposition parties.

The point on which the opposition most clearly made its influence felt was the number of representatives per province. Suárez was convinced that his supporters would run strongly in the less populated rural districts. He, therefore, wanted to assign to each province three representatives plus one or more according to population. This would have meant that the smallest provinces would have four representatives. Since there are fifty provinces in addition to Ceuta and Melilla and there would be only 350 seats, fewer than 150 seats would be available for distribution among the more heavily populated provinces. The opposition, which expected to do well in the large cities, vigorously opposed this plan. The final arrangement granted each province two representatives plus at least one in proportion to its population. This still meant that the rural constituencies, where the right and center hoped to do best, were heavily overrepresented. The province of Soria had one deputy for every 33,000 inhabitants, while Madrid had 140,000 inhabitants for each deputy. The fifteen smallest provinces, with 3.4 million inhabitants, would have 53 seats. Barcelona, with 4.5 million inhabitants, would have only 33 seats. Nonetheless, the disproportion would have been even more severe had the pressure of the opposition not forced Suárez to modify his original plan.

In order to favor the creation of large parties and avoid fragmentation in the Cortes, the law required a party to obtain at least three percent of the vote in a given province in order to win a seat. More important, it provided for a highly modified form of proportional representation following the system devised by d'Hondt. The requirements established for gaining access to the state-owned television also excluded parties too small to present complete lists of candidates in at least half the provinces.

In the election for the lower house, voting was by closed and blocked lists. Each party presented a ranked list of as many candidates as the province was to have deputies, from the minimum of three to the maximum of 34 in Barcelona. The voter chose the list he preferred, but could not indicate personal preferences for one particular candidate over another.

In the election for the Senate, the voters could choose the names they wished to vote for out of a single list of candidates proposed by all parties as well as independents. Victory would go to the four candidates with the largest number of votes, a system which favored candidates backed by very large parties or alliances.

The general effect of this legislation, which was passed by decree-law in mid-March, was to favor the large parties or coalitions of parties that could most easily make themselves heard in the press. The decree was, therefore, accepted with very little public protest. Only after the elections would some critics begin to point out the inequities of the system and the way in which it favored the conservative center-right.

THE LEGALIZATION OF PARTIES AND THE AMNESTY

During the first eight months of the Suárez government, the only legal parties were those of the right. The rest were either illegal, like the Communist Party and the groups to its left, or tolerated but without any legal status. The legislation on political parties proposed by the Arias government and approved by the Cortes in June 1976, granted the government great discretionary power in the legalization of parties. Groups wishing legal authorization had to apply to the Ministry of the Interior, which would rule on the merits of each case. The very broad wording of the law would have justified refusing authorization to almost any party of the left. All the parties of the left and center-left denounced this legislation as anti-democratic and refused to request authorization. They demanded automatic legal recognition of all political parties as a precondition for participation in the elections.

Although the opposition's statements were always phrased in terms of granting automatic authorization to *all* parties, the key question was the legalization of the Communist Party. Ever since the creation of the Democratic Junta, but especially since the meeting of its Central Committee in Rome in July 1976, the PCE had concentrated all its efforts on obtaining legal status and public recognition of its legitimacy. It stressed its commitment to "multiparty democratic government" and argued that no system which denies legal status to the Communist Party can properly be called democratic.

Throughout the fall and winter of 1976, the PCE took one step after another to assert its presence on the Spanish scene and to force the government to recognize its right to participate in the political process. In November, members of its executive committee publicly handed out party membership cards in Madrid until arrested by the police. Early in December, Santiago Carrillo, who had been refused permission to enter the country, held a clandestine news conference in which he announced plans to present a slate of candidates in the upcoming election.

A few weeks later Carrillo, together with six other members of the executive committee, was arrested on a street in northern Madrid. He had been living in Spain since February. The government appeared embarrassed by his arrest, which apparently had not been ordered by the Ministry of the Interior, and which provoked vigorous protests from the entire left. Shortly before the new year, Carrillo and the other members of the executive committee were set free on bail, with a tacit understanding that they would not be brought to trial. In this way, the government in effect recognized the Communist leader's right to remain in the country. Early in January, the opposition announced that Carrillo would represent the Communists on the committee negotiating with Suárez, while the Party proclaimed its complete concurrence with the French Communist Party's assertion that the doctrine of the dictatorship of the proletariat was now outdated.

The opposition and the PCE itself succeeded in creating a climate of opinion in which legalization of the Communist Party became the touchstone of the government's democratic character. It was beginning to appear that most of the left and center-left parties would actually refuse to participate in the elections if the government did not modify the law on political parties to permit legalization of the PCE. Suárez and King Juan Carlos were reluctant to recognize the PCE, less because of its potential electoral strength than because of fear of strong army reactions. In early February 1977, however, the government finally gave in to opposition demands and announced new legislation on political parties by which it deprived itself of discretionary power in their legalization. Under the new legislation, applications for legal recognition had to be approved within ten days or be sent to the Supreme Court. The decision was thus taken out of the hands of the government and transferred to the Court.

The legislation was a complete success in inducing the major opposition parties to accept legal status and participate in the elections. Without waiting to see what the actual fate of the Communist Party would be, all major political groups which had not yet done so, immediately applied for legal status. The Spanish Communist Party itself wasted no time in filing an application. On February 22, the government forwarded the case to the Supreme Court. Suárez may well have hoped that the Court would find in favor of the PCE, but whatever its decision, he would not be held responsible for it.

While the Court deliberated, the PCE and its allies continued to press their case. Early in March Enrico Berlinguer and Georges Marchais came to Madrid for a "Eurocommunist summit." In his statement at the airport, the Secretary General of the French Communist Party declared that he had come "to express our solidarity with the PCE and to request its legalization."

To Suárez's surprise and dismay, on April 1 the Supreme Court ruled that the question was not judicial but political, and as such an issue to be decided by the government, not the courts. The maneuver which had seemed so well designed for avoiding the responsibility of a decision had failed entirely. The government was now faced once again with the question it had hoped to avoid. On April 9, it bit the bullet and announced that the PCE would be registered as a political party.

This decision provoked the resignation of the Minister of the Navy, Admiral Gabriel Pita da Veiga, the only remaining minister to have been named by Franco. Although the only other resignation was that of Admiral Enrique Amador Franco, Under Secretary of the Merchant Marine, other high-ranking officers were upset by the decision. The Supreme Council of the Army held a stormy meeting at the end of which it approved a resolution noting its "repulsion" at the government's decision, which the army accepted only out of patriotism. The officers also advised the government that the army was "indissolubly united in defense of the unity of the fatherland, of the flag, of the permanence of the Crown, and of the good name and discipline of the army."

The crisis was a serious one, but the fact that the army did accept, however grudgingly, the legalization of the Communist Party, demonstrated dramatically the success of the efforts made by King Juan Carlos, President Suárez, and General Gutiérrez Mellado to gain control over the armed forces by replacing ultra-conservative commanders with more liberal ones. Among the most influential voices in favor of the government's position during the crisis was Lieutenant General Antonio Ibáñez Freire, named head of the Civil Guard only a few months earlier. King Juan Carlos's close, friendly relations with senior military officers served to reassure them and made them accept a decision which might otherwise have provoked a coup or at least a call by the army for Suárez's resignation.

The army's discontent with the decision in favor of the Communist Party was the most important factor in the government's subsequent refusal to recognize the extreme-left parties like the Workers' Revolutionary Organization and the Marxist-Leninist Communist Party prior to the elections. These were miniscule groups whose claim to legal status received no support from the Communists, Socialists, or Christian Democrats and whose cause the liberal press did not espouse. In the absence of strong pressure in their favor, Suárez chose not to grant them legal status so as not to further irritate the army. By May 6, the Interior Ministry had registered 156 parties, but 67 others remained unregistered and were therefore unable to take part in the elections in their own name, though some did present "independent" candidates.

The amnesty granted in July 1976 had not extended to political prisoners found guilty of or being held on charges of crimes involving violence against persons, whether or not they were directly involved in them. In addition, the ongoing political terrorism in the Basque country and in other parts of Spain was steadily increasing the number of political prisoners. Throughout the fall and winter there were repeated demonstrations, especially in the Basque country, calling for total amnesty for all political prisoners, including those jailed after July 1976. The size and frequency of the demonstrations showed that further measures were necessary if a climate of reconciliation was to be formed for the elections.

On March 11, the Council of Ministers announced a new amnesty and pardon together with a promise to review the cases of those who did not benefit from the new general measures. It promised to free all persons excluded from the July 1976 amnesty who had not been the actual authors of violence against persons as long as their cooperation had not been necessary or direct. Sentences for political crimes committed between July 1976 and the referendum of December 15, 1976 would be reduced by 12 years. The cases of all political prisoners not freed as a result of one of the previous measures would be considered individually, with the possibility of obtaining a pardon or conditional liberty. Finally, all other sentences were reduced by one-fourth.

Several hundred prisoners were set free as a result of these measures. By early May, only 23 Basque political prisoners remained in jail: 15 awaiting trial and 8 sentenced for crimes of violence. Nonetheless, the Basque country continued to be the scene of massive demonstrations in favor of total amnesty. After the police opened fire on pro-amnesty demonstrators in Rentería on May 12, killing one person, an estimated 200,000 people walked off their jobs in Guipúzcoa province. Days later a general strike paralyzed Vizcaya province. To guarantee a minimum of calm for the elections, and to insure that the Basques would not abstain in the general election, as they had done in the December referendum, on May 20 the government offered to allow the remaining Basques being held in prison to go into exile. The measure was successful in restoring some order in the region, although less than half the prisoners accepted expatriation and many of those who did so soon returned to Spain.

PUBLIC ORDER

More bloodshed accompanied moderate reform from above in Spain than revolution from below in Portugal. Between Franco's death and the June 1977 elections, 67 persons died in political violence. The government had to cope with violence from the extreme left, the extreme right, its own police forces, and Basque nationalists.

Violence ebbed and flowed continuously, but in January 1977 it reached a crest which seemed to endanger the existence of the government and of the entire project of moderate reform. The country was already edgy because of the unresolved kidnapping of Antonio María de Oriol y Urquijo, the conservative president of the Advisory Council of State, abducted from his Madrid office by the First of October Anti-Fascist Resistance Group (GRAPO) four days before the referendum. The seeming inability of the police to come up with any solid leads in the case had incensed the extreme right and caused a widespread sense of uneasiness and lack of confidence in the government's ability to control the situation.

The crisis began on Sunday, January 23, when a young student was shot down by ultra-rightists during a pro-amnesty rally in Madrid. The following morning Lieutenant General Emilio Villaescusa Quilis, President of the Supreme Council of Military Justice and former Army Chief of Staff, was kidnapped by GRAPO, which still held Oriol y Urquijo. Another student involved in a demonstration in Madrid died Monday afternoon, a few hours after being hit by a police tear gas canister. Before the evening was over, a group of men armed with submachine guns broke into the Madrid office of a number of Communist labor lawyers, killing four men and leaving five others seriously wounded, of whom one died shortly thereafter. The following day tens of thousands of workers struck in Madrid and Barcelona to protest rightist violence. The police reported the arrest of a large number of rightist activists, including many foreign Fascists. The Communist Party staged an impressive funeral for the victims of the attack on the lawyers' offices. Some 50,000 persons filed through the streets of Madrid in quiet and orderly fashion with Communist militants acting as marshals.

In the face of a growing wave of strikes protesting the violence, the government prohibited all further demonstrations and announced its intention to make use of the special powers of search and arrest contemplated in the anti-terrorist decree of August 1975. On Friday, January 28, violence broke out again in Madrid. Shortly before noon two gunmen entered a postal savings bank and shot down two members of the national Armed Police. A few hours later three gunmen killed one Civil Guard and seriously wounded three others with submachine guns and hand grenades, bringing the death toll in Madrid to ten from Sunday to Friday.

the mass of the Spanish people demonstrated remarkable determination to institute a freer, more liberal system of government without revolution and without capitulating to demands from the extreme right for a return to the systems of government that had guaranteed external calm during Franco's long reign. At an emergency cabinet meeting, the government suspended Articles 15 and 18 of the "Rights of Spaniards" to permit searches without previous authorization and to allow suspects to be held more than 72 hours. On January 30, Suárez appeared on television to plead for calm and to assure the public that the government would repress violence energetically without allowing itself to be driven to over-reactions. He attributed the violence to "small groups with no social backing made up of professional criminals" intent on "liquidating the political process in which we find ourselves immersed and leading the country's political forces to a violent, radical confrontation." Suárez's speech was accompanied by numerous arrests of right and left wing extremists, which stemmed, at least for the moment, the tide of rising violence.

In some cases it is difficult to know which political extreme was responsible for a particular act of violence. Many liberals and leftists, for example, charged that the apparently ultra-left October First group (GRAPO) was in fact made up of rightists attempting to stop political reform by provoking an intervention of the army. Conservatives, of course, denied that charge. More important than accurately assigning the guilt for particular acts of violence to the extreme right and left is to realize that the government in fact faced a serious challenge from both ends of the political spectrum.

The problem of dealing with violence was complicated by the difficulties of controlling the police. The training and habits of 40 years are not easily left behind, and the police at times continued to repress what they considered subversion even as the government was proceeding towards its legalization. In some cases the double standards which seemed to exist may have been due to a contradiction between the orders issued by the Ministry of the Interior and the avowed policy of the government, but in others it appears that the police acted on their own accord, ignoring or interpreting in the harshest possible sense the directives received from the government. Some individual members of the police forces were also active members of the ultra-rightist groups responsible for acts of terrorism, although it is impossible to determine the extent of such abuses.

In most of Spain, terrorism was sporadic, and declined after the crisis of January 1977. In the Basque country, however, violence was an ongoing problem for which the government could find no workable solution. It came from the extreme left and the extreme right, aided and abetted at times by the police, as well as from militant Basque nationalists, especially those who belonged to ETA. The violence which was most difficult to deal with, however, and which caused the greatest concern, was not that of small minorities of whatever political origin. The most serious problem in the Basque country was created by the bitter hostility between large parts of the population and the Civil Guard. Far more frequently than in the rest of the country, police efforts to stop or control demonstrations, marches, and strikes led to major violence. Many otherwise moderate Basques felt intense hatred for the police, who in their turn felt and acted like an occupation force in a hostile foreign country. The frequent violence which resulted, fueled the fires of Basque nationalism and complicated enormously the problem of finding an acceptable formula for Basque autonomy within a Spanish state. As we discussed in talking about amnesty, until well into May it seemed quite possible that the Basque parties would refuse to participate in the June 1977 elections and that massive abstentions would vitiate the elections there if violence did not prevent their being held altogether.

PARTY FORMATION AND THE ELECTORAL CAMPAIGN

While the government framed an electoral law, legalized political parties, extended the amnesty to virtually all political prisoners, and sought to control violence, politicians were busy forming parties and laying the groundwork for their electoral campaigns.

The original nucleus of a center coalition was the Popular Party, led by two former Franco ministers, José María de Areilza and Pío Cabanillas. The Popular Party (PP) was itself a conglomeration of center and center-right reformist politicians of liberal and right-wing Christian Democratic and Social Democratic leanings, as well as a number of former servants of Franco who were not very closely identified with his regime. Unlike the parties of the left and center-left, it requested legal recognition in October 1976 under the legislation approved during the final days of the Arias government.

In January 1977, the PP formed a loose electoral alliance called Democratic Center (CD) with a number of other liberal and Christian Democratic parties. The most important were the Federation of Democratic and Liberal Parties of Joaquín Garrigues Walker, the Christian Democratic Party of Fernando Alvarez de Miranda, the Spanish Democratic Union of Alberto Monreal Luque, the Liberal Party of Enrique Larroque, and the Popular Democratic Party of Ignacio Camuñas. They were joined in February by the Social Democratic Grouping of Francisco Fernández Ordóñez.

From its inception, the Democratic Center had the support and encouragement of Suárez, who considered the political organization of the center essential to stopping the growth of the Francoist Popular Alliance (AP) on the right and of the Socialists on the left. It was probably with Suárez's backing that Pío Cabanillas won election in early February as president of the Popular Party, defeating Areilza, who enjoyed much more popularity and had been considered the party's dominant figure. If Suárez were already thinking of taking over the Democratic Center for his own purposes, Cabanillas was a far less formidable future opponent than Areilza. After allowing a decent interval, Areilza resigned altogether from the Popular Party and effectively withdrew from active politics. Soon Pio Cabanillas also felt himself being elbowed aside.

Suárez did not commit himself to the Democratic Center until the very last moment. Not until April 28 did he say that he intended to run for election. By this time, however, he was already negotiating actively with the Democratic Center. In return for his support, he demanded the right to place his own candidates on the CD's electoral lists, even though they might not belong to any of its constituent parties. His right-hand man, Leopoldo Calvo Sotelo, was responsible for putting at the head of the lists some 80 "independents," relatively young men who had served the Franco regime in the bureaucracy and who were now reliable supporters of Suárez's reform from above.

Even after the leaders of the CD agreed to this price, which forced them to sacrifice the electoral hopes of many of their own supporters and protégés, Suárez refused to commit himself formally. Right up to the last day for registering electoral coalitions, he kept open the option of forming a coalition of his own which would include CD and other elements as well. Only on May 4 did he announce over television his intention of running as the first candidate in Madrid of the Center Democratic Union (UCD), which was registered that same day. The official representative of the renamed coalition would not be Cabanillas but Suárez's man, Calvo Sotelo.

The UCD's campaign took maximum advantage of Suárez's popularity. Posters with enormous color photos of the President proclaimed: "A Vote for the Center is a Vote for Suárez." Unlike most other groups, the UCD did not hold mass rallies. It depended instead on advertisements and on television. Its propaganda was low-keyed and determinedly un-ideological. The UCD promised voters that it would democratize and reform Spanish political life at the same time as it guaranteed continuity of government and administration and unwavering support of the monarchy. Correctly perceiving that most of its potential voters did not want to think about the past, either to criticize or to praise it, the UCD attempted to ignore Franco and the Francoist past of many of its candidates. It offered both change and security, but laid more stress on security than on change. This emphasis was, perhaps, inevitable in light of the close ties of many UCD candidates with the Franco regime.

The Spanish Socialist Workers Party (PSOE) failed to unify all Socialists before the election. The Historical Spanish Socialist Workers'

Party (PSOE[h]), the Popular Socialist Party (PSP), and the Federation of Socialist Parties (FPS) refused its advances. The PSOE(h) chose to run in a coalition with the Spanish Social Democratic Party, and the PSP and FSP formed a coalition of their own, ironically enough called Socialist Unity Coalition. Nonetheless, the PSOE was clearly the most important Socialist party and the one which received the recognition and support of other European Socialists.

The PSOE's political line was set at its 27th Congress, held in Madrid in December 1976. At that time the party still enjoyed no legal existence. Suárez had denied it permission to hold a congress in Madrid in the fall, for fear that granting permission might endanger the Cortes's approval of his reform measures. Only after the reform had passed the Cortes did the government authorize the PSOE to hold its first congress in Spain since the Civil War.

The moderate sector of the party's leadership dominated the congress, reelecting Felipe González as First Secretary and choosing Alfonso Guerra as Organizational Secretary. The radical former First Secretary, Pablo Castellano, was excluded altogether from the congress, and Gregorio Peces-Barba was defeated by Guerra in his bid for Organizational Secretary. The party emerged from the congress with a leadership that was significantly less radical than its base.

The program approved during the 27th Congress defined the PSOE as a class party and its ideology as Marxian Socialist, specifically rejecting social democracy. There was little in the Socialist campaign, however, that would have offended a European Social Democrat. The PSOE's campaign rhetoric was far less radical than its December program. It projected the image of a reformist party, the logical option for Spaniards of all classes who wanted a change in the political direction of their country without revolutionary adventures. The campaign capitalized heavily on the personal charisma of the handsome 34-year-old González. Party orators frequently invoked the PSOE's glorious history and its ties with the great Spanish Socialist leaders of the early twentieth century.

Other European Socialist parties lent their support to the PSOE. Willy Brandt, Olof Palme, Pietro Nenni, Michael Foote, and François Mitterand all attended the 27th Congress. German Socialists provided technical assistance and advice throughout the campaign. Close ties with the major European Socialist parties helped give the PSOE a European and social democratic image which won it the support of many moderate voters who felt uncomfortable with the UCD because of its excessive connection with the Franco regime but who were equally anxious to avoid revolutionary adventures.

The Spanish Communist Party entered the electoral campaign with clear advantages and disadvantages. During the long years of the Franco regime it had maintained its own organization more successfully than any other opposition group. Its leadership was coherent, experienced, and highly disciplined. In addition, the Workers' Commissions, with which it had close ties, represented a potential mass of members. On the negative side, it faced the bitter hostility not only of conservatives but of many members of the Spanish left who had been persecuted by Communists during the Civil War and who continued to mistrust them. In view of this situation, in the June 1977 election, the PCE was less anxious to win a large number of seats in the Cortes than to gain recognition as a legitimate actor on the political scene.

The Central Committee, meeting in Madrid in mid-April 1977, days after the party's legalization, announced its decision to abandon the Republican flag the PCE had regularly used at its meetings and to adopt in its place the red and gold Spanish national flag associated with the monarchy. Carrillo declared that his party had observed the instauration of the monarchy with serious reservations, but that "the facts were demonstrating that under the monarchy we are moving toward democracy. . . . The choice today is not between monarchy and republic, but between dictatorship and democracy."

Speaking under a large banner that proclaimed "A Vote for Communism is a Vote for Democracy," the Secretary General of the PCE noted that "our path is in fact narrow and any unconsidered act can provoke catastrophic reactions for Spain and for democracy." PCE militants were ordered not to organize mass demonstrations celebrating their legalization, and throughout the spring party leaders made every effort to avoid provoking the army or the extreme right.

The electoral program approved at the April meeting of the Central Committee was very carefully worded, laying major stress on consolidating democratic freedoms rather than on social reform. Communist leaders pointed to their long history of opposition to the Franco Regime as the guarantee of their sincere democratic convictions in contrast to the recent converts who abounded in other parts of the political spectrum. During the campaign, the party sought to avoid being associated with violence or extremism. It refused, for instance, to support a general strike in the Basque country during May on the grounds that it would needlessly increase tension in an already divided country. Carrillo insistently preached his moderate brand of Eurocommunism, but he was embarrassed by occasional statements from the 82-year-old "Pasionaria" describing Eurocommunism as "pure foolishness" and confessing that she had always been pro-Soviet. The right also accused him of atrocities during the Civil War. Nonetheless, the campaign was well run and helped to make the PCE seem a respectable party that could be relied on to support democracy in Spain.

At the other end of the political spectrum stood the Popular Alliance (AP), an electoral coalition comprising seven different groups formed under Arias's legislation permitting political associations. Its leaders were former ministers and well-known political figures of the Franco era. They were, on the average, fifteen to twenty years older than those of the UCD and had occupied more important positions in the Franco administration.

The AP distinguished itself from the ultra-right like the New Force by admitting the need for political and constitutional reform, and by renouncing the use of violence. It criticized Suárez and his government for allowing public order to deteriorate and for failing to protect the unity of Spain as well as for permitting a growing economic and social crisis. Among its favorite slogans was: "Under Franco We Lived Better."

The AP seemed at first a formidable group. The personal fame of many of its leaders and the economic resources it commanded led most observers to believe that it would win a sizeable number of votes from people concerned primarily with the maintenance of law and order. Its campaign was dominated by Fraga Irribarne. Completely abandoning his former claims to represent the moderate center-right, Fraga closely identified himself with the Franco regime and bitterly denounced the "treason" that was opening Spain to Marxism. Failing to recognize the country's intense desire for reconciliation and peace, he preached a crusade which found little echo among the public. The violent tone of AP's campaign alienated many sincere proponents of order who increasingly saw AP itself as representing a real threat to the future peace of Spain.

Christian Democracy had been weakened by the changes that had occurred in Europe and in the Catholic Church during the prior thirty years. Like other Europeans, many Spaniards gradually ceased to see an immediate Communist threat to their security and therefore saw little need for a strong Christian Democracy as a bulwark against Communism. The Church was wary of being identified with any single party and was no longer willing to use its considerable resources to back Christian Democracy. Despite these problems, Spanish Christian Democrats might have been more successful had they not mismanaged their campaign and misjudged their electorate.

Numerous attempts to create a single unified Christian Democratic Party failed because of personal rivalries and an excessive stress on ideological purity. José María Gil Robles adamantly refused to recognize the Christian Democratic credentials of groups he judged tainted with Francoist associations, thereby driving them into the arms of the UCD, which orthodox Christian Democrats were not allowed to join. Largely under the influence of Joaquín Ruiz Jiménez, the editor of the left Catholic *Cuadernos para el diálogo*, the Christian Democrats who did not join the UCD directed their campaign mostly to the center-left, disdaining the center-right where their natural clientele lay.

The campaign in the Basque country had characteristics of its own. As in the rest of Spain, political groups and parties proliferated during the year and a half between Franco's death and the elections. Until early 1977, the parties which classified themselves as *abertzales*, that is purely Basque parties not subordinate to any larger Spanish group, seemed to dominate the scene. They encountered considerable success in their efforts to pose as the sole legitimate representatives of Basque interests, even though virtually all parties that presented candidates in the Basque country defended autonomy in one form or another.

The traditional Basque Nationalist Party (PNV) had dominated Basque politics during the Republic. Now it combined centrist economic and social policies and an interclass character typical of Christian Democrats with vigorous defense of Basque autonomy. It called for the immediate restitution of the statute of autonomy granted to the Basques by the Republic in 1936. To the left of the PVN there appeared a plethora of parties ranging from Social Democrats through Socialists to Marxist-Leninists which combined their various social and economic policies with a call for Basque autonomy and in some cases independence.

The campaign centered chiefly around local issues. Throughout Spain politicians concentrated their attention on political issues, leaving in the background social and economic ones. In the Basque country the range of issues was further narrowed to Basque autonomy and amnesty for political prisoners.

Some extremist *abertzale* groups, including ETA V, spoke in favor of total independence for the Basque country, although even they presented it as a long-range goal and called for autonomy within Spain as an immediate solution. The larger *abertzale* groups, including the PNV, the Basque Socialist Party (ESB), and the Basque Nationalist Action Party (ANV), rejected all talk of independence and focused their attention on demanding more autonomy, starting with the restitution of the rights granted by the 1936 autonomy statute.

The *abertzales* were joined in these demands by almost all the other parties. The PSOE stressed its commitment to a federal structure for Spain, within which the Basque country could easily find its proper place. The Communist Party of Euzkadi also proposed a federal constitution for Spain, and as a short-term solution suggested the reinstatement of the 1936 statute. The UCD rejected federalism, but proclaimed its commitment to regional autonomy for all regions whose history, geography, and economic situation might lead them to desire it.

The UCD was vague and cautious in its declarations about autonomy and seemed to be moved more by the requirements of electoral politics than by any principled commitment to decentralization. The PSOE hammered away at its proposals for a federal constitutional structure, but deliberately avoided hard questions about how to reconcile regional fiscal

autonomy with demands for a more equitable income distribution between rich and poor regions. The *abertzale* parties were all clearly pledged
to Basque autonomy, but the PNV was markedly more moderate in its
demands than the extreme left groups of recent formation.

Full amnesty for political prisoners overshadowed even the question
of autonomy. Police and demonstrators clashed repeatedly as frequent,
often violent, amnesty demonstrations shook the region. The issue of
amnesty united the majority of the Basque population against the government at Madrid and threatened for a time to lead to massive Basque
abstention in the general elections similar to that in the December 1976
referendum. Only the Suárez government's decision to allow the few
remaining Basque political prisoners to go into exile succeeded temporarily in calming public anger and convinced most Basque parties to urge
their members to vote.

During the final weeks of the campaign the smaller *abertzale* parties
lost ground. In all four provinces, the PSOE ran a very active campaign,
appealing to the working class and especially to the numerous immigrants
from other regions. In Guipúzcoa and Vizcaya the PNV was also very
visible. In the other two Basque provinces, Alava and Navarre, the PNV
failed to generate enthusiasm for its brand of conservative Basque nationalism. In these two provinces, voters who did not gravitate toward one
of the major parties, supported one of the numerous ultra-left splinter
groups, most of which included a specifically Basque element in their
platforms, but the PSOE and the UCD dominated the campaign.

In Catalonia, the proliferation of political parties and groups was at
first even greater than in the Basque country. At one point, over a
hundred existed. Only the need to unite for the upcoming elections
finally brought about a reduction in their number and made it possible to
draw an orderly picture of Catalan political forces.

The climate of the electoral campaign in Catalonia was far less
agitated and violent than in the Basque country. Since there were no
Catalan political prisoners, the question of amnesty did not bulk large,
and there was never any probability that the Catalans would refuse to take
part in the election. Barcelona saw far less political violence in the months
preceding the election than did Bilbao or even San Sebastián whose
population is only about one-tenth as large.

As in the Basque country, regional autonomy was a dominant theme
in most political speeches in Catalonia during the electoral campaign. No
party that showed any strength in the region failed to support it. Catalans
tended to form purely regional parties, without any formal ties to national
organizations, although as the elections approached, they made important alliances with national parties.

The right was occupied principally by a Catalan version of the
Popular Alliance, headed by the former Commissar of the Plan of Economic Development, Laureano López Rodó. Despite his Francoist past,

López Rodó laid heavy stress on his personal ties with the region and spoke with fervor about Catalan autonomy.

The center of the political spectrum was occupied by three groups. The UCD and the Christian Democrats took no special interest in Catalonia. Their organization and campaign followed the same patterns there as in the rest of the country, except for a heavier stress on regional autonomy. The distinctive Catalan center party was the Democratic Pact for Catalonia (PDC), which had no ties with Spanish national parties. Its founders were Ramón Trias Fargas, an economist, and Jordi Pujol, a banker who supported social democratic economic and social policies and who had been a leader of Catalan opposition to Franco. Pujol was a moderate, pragmatic politician, anxious to integrate into Catalonia its immigrant working class population and extremely popular with the Catalan middle class.

The largest and most interesting political force in Catalonia was the electoral alliance called Socialists of Catalonia (SC). Joan Reventós formed SC by uniting under his own leadership his purely Catalan Socialist Party with the Catalan section of the PSOE. Many political experts predicted that no group "franchised" by a national party would succeed in Catalonia. The SC was working under another handicap since it could not count on a strong historical tradition in a region which had been an anarchist stronghold during the Republic. Nonetheless, the alliance proved very successful. Reventós's long-standing defense of Catalonia's special status was sufficiently well known to offset in the eyes of native Catalan voters the demerits of his alliance with the Catalan branch of the PSOE, while that alliance won him the confidence of many immigrants from Andalucía in Barcelona's working-class districts.

The extreme left was represented in Catalonia by the Unified Socialist Party of Catalonia (PSUC) and by the Catalan Left (EC). The first is the Catalan branch of the PCE. Despite its distinctive name the PSUC is a perfectly orthodox Communist party, with strong ties to the national organization in which it is fully represented. It enjoyed in Catalonia a particularly solid and highly developed organization as well as a number of well-known leaders like Gregorio López Raimundo and Jordi Solé Tura. The Catalan Left is a heterogeneous left-wing alliance, including Catalan Republicans and the Leninist/Maoist Spanish Work Party.

The peculiar characteristics of this campaign must be taken into account in assessing the results of the elections. The entire campaign had a certain air of a plebiscite on democracy. Party programs were vague and offered few specific proposals in the areas of economic and social policy. The voters seemed even less interested than the politicians in concrete programs. They were swayed principally by personalities and by the parties' images as more or less democratic, more or less reformist. Suárez could point to his record as the President of the Government during the previous year, but other leaders could offer no concrete achievements.

The parties lacked structure. To a large extent they were casual alliances of like-thinking men rather than organizations designed to mobilize voter support. Most had been formed only a few weeks or months before the official campaign opened. Even those like the PCE and the PSOE that had existed for a long time had experienced such rapid growth and such profound changes that in many ways they were still in their formative stages. The largest party, the UCD, was not formally a party at all but an electoral coalition of parties with quite diverse ideologies and with competing leaderships. No party, including the UCD, was well enough organized to present a slate of candidates in all 52 electoral circumscriptions.

The UCD spent the most money on the electoral campaign, approximately $10 million. The next-largest spender was the AP, whose expenditures amounted to almost $8 million. The PSOE spent approximately $4 million, and the PCE a little over $1.5 million. Expenditures per seat won in the two houses ranged from a high of almost $500,000 for the AP to a low of only $22,000 for the Socialists of Catalonia. Each seat cost the UCD about $37,000, while the costs for the PSOE and the PCE were $31,000 and $133,000 respectively.

The official campaign was brief. Even well-organized parties would have found it difficult to get their message across to the voters in a month and a half. The campaigns conducted by weak and disorganized parties failed to reach many Spaniards at all. Three weeks before the election, 14 percent of people polled still had not decided whether to vote or not, and 57 percent of those who intended to vote still had not decided which party to support.

Press coverage of the campaign was ample but uneven in scope and quality. Except for the large Barcelona dailies and some papers in the Basque country, most newspapers concentrated heavily on national affairs, paying scant attention to local or regional problems or candidates. Reporting and analysis on the larger political and constitutional issues that dominated the campaign was generally on a low level except for *La Vanguardia* in Barcelona and *ABC, Informaciones, El País,* and *Ya* in Madrid. News weeklies such as *Cambio 16* and opinion journals such as *Cuadernos para el diálogo* and *El Socialista* supplemented the daily press but reached only a small segment of the population.

The press exercised considerable influence on the politicians, especially in the campaign for amnesty, but it is easy to exaggerate its influence on the mass of voters. Except on rare days, even the Sunday editions of the largest newspapers barely reach 200,000 copies. Only a small minority outside Madrid and Barcelona ever reads one of the national papers. According to a May 1977 survey, only 9 percent of the adult population reads any newspaper on a daily basis, and 50 percent never reads anything at all.

In contrast, important television programs draw as many as 13 million viewers. Even the staid and closely controlled evening news broadcasts are regularly seen by three to five million. For half the population they are the only source of news. Access to television was, therefore, the single most important factor in the campaign. Since Spanish television is state-owned and operated, the opposition feared it would be used by the government exclusively to promote its own candidates. The government finally offered three ten-minute spots to any party that presented a full slate of candidates in 25 or more of Spain's 50 provinces. This gave smaller groups no chance to present their message and even the larger parties which met this criterion were far from having equal access to television. News programs regularly covered the activities of Suárez and other UCD candidates but virtually ignored the speeches and statements of opposition candidates. Since Spanish television would not accept paid political announcements, the opposition was limited to its allotted 30 minutes. Greater television exposure contributed importantly to the UCD victory.

THE ELECTIONS

The elections were held in an atmosphere of surprising calm, marred by few incidents. Numerous minor irregularities occurred in casting and counting the votes, but most were due to lack of familiarity with the process or to incompetence rather than to deliberate attempts to falsify the results. Reporting of the electoral results was very slow and erratic. The government deliberately delayed announcing the vote in districts in which the Socialists had done exceptionally well until it had other results to offset them. When it began to become clear that the Socialists had won almost as many votes as the UCD, television stopped announcing the popular vote and concentrated exclusively on the number of seats since the UCD's margin was much greater there. Despite delays and manipulation of the news, however, the final outcome was accurately reported. On balance, the elections were the most free and most honest ever held in Spain, and their results reflect accurately the choices of the voters on June 15.

Parts of this section are based upon material that will appear in *Spain after Polls*, Howard Pennimann, ed., Washington, D.C.: American Enterprise Institute for Public Policy Research. To be published.

Of the eligible voters, 78.3 percent went to the polls (the highest percentage in any free Spanish election in the twentieth century), and only 0.2 percent cast blank ballots. Despite the large number of parties present on the ballot, the vote was highly concentrated. Most voters resisted the temptation to support slightly more congenial ideological positions in order to back groups which seemed likely to play a major role in the country's future. Between them, the Center Democratic Union and the Spanish Socialist Workers' Party won almost two-thirds of the popular vote for the Congress of Deputies. The four major parties took more than 80 percent of the vote, and small parties other than Catalan and Basque regional ones accounted for only about 13.5 percent.

Ballots were cast separately for senators and deputies. The elections for the Senate are more difficult to analyze and far less revealing since voters were free to choose among individual candidates, rather than only among parties, and since numerous special coalitions and alliances were formed at the provincial and regional levels. The most important facts about the senatorial elections are that the Center Democratic Union won a small absolute majority of the 207 popularly elected senators, and that the king's appointment of 41 senators strengthened the ranks of the center and the right, guaranteeing the UCD's control of the Senate. We will center our attention here exclusively on the results in the election of deputies (see Table 4.1).

Most center and rightist voters supported the Center Democratic Union. It won by a large margin in many rural areas and small towns throughout Spain, but the geographic center of the country and Galicia were its strongholds. Its best showing was in the Canary Islands province of Las Palmas where it received 69 percent of the vote, followed by Suárez's home province of Avila with 67.5 percent. In 36 of Spain's 50 provinces it won a majority or plurality. It outdistanced the Socialists in Madrid by a mere 0.7 percent (32.2 percent to 31.5 percent) and in Spain's other three largest cities it lost to them. Its worst defeat was in Barcelona where it received only 15.1 percent. Within the UCD, 56 seats went to the "independent" candidates whom Suárez had placed at the head of many provincial lists as the price of his entering the coalition. The Popular Party of Pío Cabinillas won 33; the Christian Democrats of Alvarez de Miranda, 16; the Social Democrats of Fernández Ordóñez, 16; the Liberals of Garrigues Walker, 16; and other groups, 28.

The Spanish Socialist Workers' Party dominated the left. It ran best in the south and in the large cities, but nowhere did it achieve an absolute majority. Its best showing was in Málaga where it received 39.1 percent of the vote. There and in eight other provinces, including Barcelona, Seville, and Valencia, it won a plurality.

TABLE 4.1

Election to Congress of Deputies, June 1977

Party or Coalition	Percent Popular Vote	Number of Seats	Percent of Seats	Index of Over- or Under-Representation[a]
Center Democratic Union (UCD)	34.7	165	47.1	+0.36
Spanish Socialist Workers' Party (PSOE)[b]	29.2	118	33.7	+0.15
Spanish Communist Party (PCE)[c]	9.2	20	5.7	−0.38
Popular Alliance (AP)	8.4	16	4.6	−0.45
United Socialists (PSP-FPS)	4.5	6	1.7	−0.62
Democratic Pact for Catalonia (PDC)	3.0	11	3.1	+0.03
Basque Nationalist Party (PNV)	1.3	8	2.3	+0.77
Catalan Christian Democracy (UCiDC)	0.7	2	0.6	−0.14
Independent Centrists	0.7	2	0.6	−0.14
Left Democratic Front (FDI)	1.4	1	0.3	−0.79
Left of Euzkadi (EE) and Other Extreme Left	0.9	1	0.3	−0.66
Christian Democracy (DC)	1.4	0	0.0	−1.0
Others	4.6	0	0.0	−1.0
	100.0	350	100.0	

[a]Index = (% Seats − % Votes) / (% Votes).
[b]Includes Socialists of Catalonia (SC).
[c]Includes Unified Socialist Party of Catalonia (PSUC).
Source: Author's elaboration from data published in *El País* (Madrid), July 17, 1977.

The election confirmed the weakness of Francoism as a political appeal. The voters were willing to close their eyes to the Francoist background of Suárez and many of his associates in the UCD because they proclaimed their new democratic faith and remained prudently silent about the past. The Popular Alliance, however, whose candidates included many of the leading figures of the final decade of the Franco regime, received only 8.4 percent of the vote. Carlos Arias Navarro failed in his attempt to win election to the Senate from Madrid, and Laureano López Rodó barely managed to win a seat as a deputy for Barcelona. The belligerent extreme right Francoists of the openly fascist variety failed to elect a single senator or deputy.

The Communist Party achieved a respectable showing thanks to its strength in Catalonia. The province of Barcelona alone accounted for 28 percent, and the four Catalan provinces for 37 percent of the total Communist vote in Spain. Communist leaders had hoped for more than the 9 percent of the vote they actually won, but they achieved their primary goal in the election of establishing the party as a legitimate participant in Spanish politics.

The great beneficiary of the electoral system was the UCD, which won almost half of the seats although it had only slightly more than one-third of the popular votes. The Socialists received a slightly higher percentage of seats than of votes, but all other national parties were penalized by the system. In the resulting chamber, the UCD's 165 seats fell just 11 short of an absolute majority of 176. The PSOE with 118 deputies had almost six times as many as its next rival, the Spanish Communist Party (see Figure 4.1).

In the Basque country, despite fears that the ETA might unleash a new campaign of violence, the elections took place in an atmosphere of calm, marred only by a few minor incidents. Voter participation in the region as a whole (76.6 percent) was only slightly lower than the national average (79.2 percent). In Guipúzcoa province, where only 71.8 percent of eligible voters cast ballots, abstention represented a protest against the government's refusal to legalize extreme left Basque political parties, and against its policy with respect to autonomy. On balance, however, the salient fact was a high index of participation pointing toward at least momentary willingness of the public and of the parties to make use of the established political framework to achieve Basque goals.

The PSOE showed unexpected strength in the Basque region, where it ran almost as well as in the country as a whole, despite the stigma of being a "Spanish" party. With 25.8 percent of the vote and nine of 26 seats, it was the largest single party in the Basque country. Equally important, however, was the strength of centrist opinion in the Basque provinces. The PNV, UCD, and other center and center-right parties accounted for 44 percent of the popular vote. They elected 15 of the

FIGURE 4.1

Seats in the Congress of Deputies, June 1977

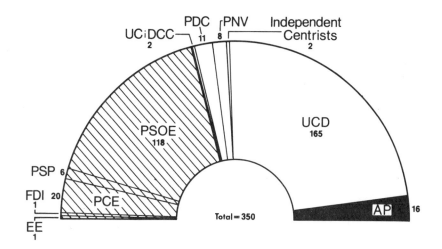

Source: *El País* (Madrid), July 17, 1977.

region's 26 deputies and accounted for more than half the seats in every province except Guipúzcoa . (See Table 4.2 and Figure 4.2.) This contrasts sharply with Catalonia and other highly industrialized parts of Spain, where the left was stronger and the center considerably weaker. The extreme left, which was awarded only one deputy, accounted for more than one-tenth of the total popular vote. Splintering into ten separate groups deprived these parties of due representation in the Cortes, but they are obviously a force to be contended with locally, especially since they have a high proportion of militants and activists.

Abertzale groups accounted for almost 40 percent of the popular vote if we include specifically Navarrese parties in the group. Thanks to the eight deputies of the PNV, *abertzale* opinion is well represented in the Cortes, but the PNV deputies stand far to the right of many Basques who voted for *abertzale* candidates of other parties. The election marked the appearance of significant left nationalist forces in the Basque country. Although they won only one seat, they deprived the right of its historic monopoly on Basque nationalism.

In Catalonia the electoral atmosphere was far less tense than in the Basque country. There was no particular reason to fear either violence or massive abstention, and in fact the elections were conducted in calm, orderly fashion.

TABLE 4.2

Basque Country—Election to Congress of Deputies, June 1977

Party or Group	Percent of Popular Vote	Number of Seats	Percent of Seats	Index of Over- or Under-representation[a]
PSOE	24.9	9	34.6	+0.39
PNV	23.4	8	30.8	+0.32
UCD	15.8	7	26.9	+0.70
Extreme Left[b]	11.0	1	3.8	−0.65
AP[c]	7.2	1	3.8	−0.47
Center Parties and Coalitions other than UCD and PNV[d]	4.8	0	0.0	−1.0
PCE	4.0	0	0.0	−1.0
Moderate *Abertzale* Left[e]	3.7	0	0.0	−1.0
PSP	1.9	0	0.0	−1.0
Other	3.3	0	0.0	−1.0

[a]Index = (% Seats − % Votes) / (% Votes).
[b]EE, FUT, AET, AETE, UNAI, Montejurra, FDI, AETNA, APN.
[c]Includes Alianza Foral in Navarre, although this group lays heavy stress on local issues and differs on some other points from AP.
[d]DCV, DIV, FDI, FNI.
[e]ESB, ANV.
Source: Author's elaboration from data published in *Diario 16* (Madrid), July 22, 1977.

The striking feature of the elections in Catalonia was the strength of the Marxist left (see Table 4.3 and Figure 4.3). The alliance between Reventós's autonomous Catalan Socialists and the PSOE paid off handsomely. Socialists of Catalonia (SC) dominated the region, taking almost a third of both its votes and seats. In addition, the Catalan version of the Communist Party (PSUC) took almost a fifth of the vote. Between them the two Marxist parties accounted for 46.6 percent of the vote, and 48.9 percent of the seats. They ran much less well in the other three provinces than in Barcelona, but the capital bulks so large that their relative weakness in other provinces did not significantly diminish their margin of victory in the region as a whole.

Jordi Pujol's Democratic Pact for Catalonia (PDC) made a respectable showing, but proved much less strong than observers had initially expected, barely surpassing the UCD in the popular vote. These two center parties taken together with the Christian Democrats accounted for 39.8 percent of the region's vote.

With the exception of the PDC, exclusively Catalan parties did not receive a large proportion of the vote, but almost all the deputies elected from Catalonia support Catalan autonomy. The lack of support for exclusively Catalan parties is a sign of the relative moderation of Catalan regional sentiment, but not of its weakness.

The election's failure to give any party a majority in the Congress of Deputies and the urgent economic and political problems facing the

FIGURE 4.2

Basque Deputies, June 1977

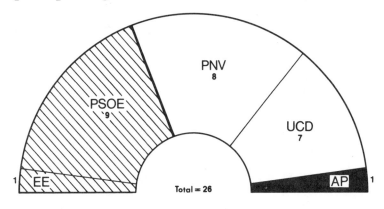

Source: El País (Madrid), July 17, 1977.
(Total: 26)

TABLE 4.3

Catalonia—Election to Congress of Deputies, June 1977

Party or Coalition	Percent of Popular Vote	Number of Seats	Percent of Seats	Index of Over- or Under-representation*
Socialists of Catalonia (SC)	28.3	15	31.9	+0.12
Unified Socialist Party of Catalonia (PSUC)	18.3	8	17.0	−0.07
Democratic Pact for Catalonia (PDC)	17.2	11	23.4	+0.36
Center Democratic Union (UCD)	16.9	9	19.1	+0.13
Center Union and Christian Democrats (UCiDC)	5.7	2	4.2	−0.26
Catalan Left (EC)	4.7	1	2.1	−0.55
Popular Alliance (AP)	3.6	1	2.1	−0.42
Other	5.2	0	0.0	−1.00

*Index = (% Seats − % Votes) / (% Votes).

Source: Author's elaboration from data published in *Diario 16* (Madrid), July 22, 1977.

FIGURE 4.3

Catalan Deputies, June 1977

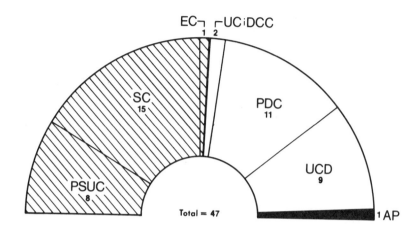

Source: *El País* (Madrid), July 17, 1977.
(Total: 47)

country led some commentators to urge the creation of a government of national unity, but neither the UCD nor the PSOE wanted to form a coalition. Suárez wished to maintain his monopoly of political power and preferred to form a cabinet made up exclusively of his own men. He was convinced that ad hoc agreements with the Catalan or Basque deputies or with the AP would allow him to pass legislation without having to construct a stable alliance with anyone. Felipe González preferred not to tie his hands and to remain in the opposition.

The outcome of the elections was extremely favorable for González's party and for the development of democracy in Spain. It firmly established the PSOE as the only serious rival of the UCD and guaranteed that the Socialist groups that had refused unification prior to the elections would have no viable alternative but to accept it now on González's terms. By remaining in the opposition, the PSOE avoided having to take responsibility for probable failures in the midst of serious political and economic difficulties. Yet the party's weight in the Congress of Deputies was sufficient to guarantee that Suárez could not ignore its wishes, especially on constitutional questions for which a broad consensus was essential.

If the UCD had won by a wide margin, Suárez would have felt less pressure to move ahead quickly with constitutional reform. If the PSOE had won the elections, King Juan Carlos would have been hard put to name a Socialist President of the Government over the opposition of the

army and of the business community. Had he exercised his legal pre-
rogative and refused to do so, he would have thrown himself into the
hands of the right and sharply reduced the chances for future democratic
reform. Had he called the Socialists to govern, the hostility of the army
would, at the very least, have kept the PSOE on a short leash politically
while the mistrust of businessmen would have led to massive flights of
capital and probably to a crippling economic crisis. Had they won the
election, the Socialists, for their part, would have encountered serious
difficulties in staffing a government. Most of the party's leaders were
young men like González, with no experience of government, nor of
legislative activity. Finding suitably qualified ministers would have been
difficult, but the real problem would have been coming up with the
hundreds of people required for the upper levels of the administration.
Socialist leaders confessed privately that they were elated by their strong
showing and pleased that they would have time to organize and acquire
experience before having to face the responsibility of government.

5

AFTER THE ELECTIONS

THE SECOND SUÁREZ GOVERNMENT

Except in the drafting of the Constitution, which we will examine in Chapter 6, the main protagonists during the months following the elections would continue to be Suárez and the leaders of the opposition parties, not the newly elected Cortes which played a relatively insignificant role in day-to-day political life. Spain still did not have a truly parliamentary system of government. Suárez was not in fact responsible to the Cortes, even after approval in November 1977 of a law providing for parliamentary responsibility. The Cortes had almost no legislative initiative. The government drafted legislation, made whatever pacts it needed with opposition parties, and manipulated the resulting parliamentary majority to get its proposals approved. Not until January 1978 did the Cortes agree for the first time to consider a proposal made by the Socialists. In this chapter, which deals with the events that formed the background of the drafting of the Constitution, we will focus our attention on Suárez and his government on the one hand, and on the opposition parties on the other. The Cortes as a body will rarely be the protagonist.

Shortly after the elections, Suárez issued a decree restructuring the government. The PSOE had called on him to give the Cortes a chance to debate any major administrative reform, but the president characteristically preferred to proceed on his own and to establish the new structure by decree. The reinstitution of a Vice President for Economic Affairs, a post which had not existed in Suárez's first government, appeared to reflect a more serious concern with economic policy. The creation of a Vice President for Defense and the simultaneous elimination of the three former armed services ministries indicated a desire to reduce military influence to a minimum. For the first time since the Civil War, a Spanish government would have only one military man among its members.

Aside from Suárez himself, only three members of the old government retained positions in the new one. Although the president's party held only a plurality of seats in the Congress of Deputies, no members of other parties were invited to join the government. All the ministers were either members of the UCD or men without any political affiliation. Five of the seven members of the Executive Committee of the UCD received ministerial portfolios. The sixth, Alvarez de Miranda, would be President of the Congress of Deputies, and the last, Leopoldo Calvo Sotelo, was expected to dedicate all his attention to transforming the UCD from a coalition into a real party.

The new government reflected the balance of forces within the UCD and the personal influence of Suárez. Before announcing the composition of the cabinet, the president consulted representatives of the other currents of the UCD, but he made the final decisions himself. Among the ministers were to be found representatives of each of the groups that constituted the UCD: Liberals, Christian Democrats, Social Democrats, and former men of the regime both from the Popular Party and from Suárez's "independents." The key positions, however, were all held by close political friends of the president.

To fill the reinstituted position of Vice President for Economic Affairs, Suárez named Professor Enrique Fuentes Quintana, a prestigious professor of public finance and fiscal law at the University of Madrid. Fuentes is a believer in a free market economy, but he is also a forthright critic of the inequities of both income and tax distribution in Spain. Suárez had offered him a ministry in his first cabinet in July 1976, but Fuentes had turned it down. He accepted now because he had been guaranteed freedom of action and the support needed to carry out his program.

The Minister of Finance, Francisco Fernández Ordóñez, a lawyer and inspector of finance, was the president of the Social Democratic Federation. If Fernández Ordóñez represented the center-left, the world of finance was represented in the economic team by three ministers: Alberto Oliart Saussol at Industry and Energy; José Lladó y Fernández-Urrutia at Transportation and Communication; and Joaquín Garrigues Walker at Public Works and Urbanism.

The only military man in the new cabinet, Lieutenant General Manuel Gutiérrez Mellado, was one of the few carry-overs from the previous cabinet. He was not popular among the senior officers of the Spanish army, but was intensely loyal to the king and had been instrumental in maintaining order and discipline during the turbulent months between the referendum and the elections. The elimination of the other armed services ministries increased his prestige by making him the sole voice of the services in the government.

For the first time in history, the Spanish government recognized the importance of the regional question by creating a position of Associate Minister for Relations with the Regions, a position filled by a 52-year-old lawyer from Seville, Manuel Clavero Arévalo, former rector of the University of Seville.

Suárez described his new government as center-left, but it was far to' the right of the Italian center-left government and would be móre accurately classified in European terms as center-right. It contained no Socialists, and its Social Democrats were really men of the center rather than of the left. Several ministers had close personal ties to the world of powerful Spanish banks, and many were reformed servants of the Franco regime who would be considered center-right or right in other European countries. The new ministers, like their predecessors, were generally young. Their average age was 45, with a range from 67 to 37.

PUBLIC ORDER

Neither holding elections nor forming a new government did anything to improve public order. The events discussed in this chapter and the next were played out against a background of terrorism and violence in the Basque country that occasionally spilled over into other parts of Spain. We will touch on some of the outstanding incidents in the course of this chapter, but it is well to remember that few weeks went by without at least one or two killings of policemen or bomb explosions.

The police for their part showed somewhat increased professionalism and restraint as time went on, but their record still left much to be desired. It was marred by several clearly unnecessary uses of firearms and other excessive force, which they justified alleging lack of adequate riot-control equipment. They also seemed incapable of preventing the growth of ordinary crime, due in large part to the rising number of unemployed youths who turned to theft or robbery.

Crime and violence in the streets were accompanied by disorder in the prisons. Conditions in many Spanish prisons were bad and the number of guards inadequate. Common criminals naturally resented being excluded from the repeated amnesties, by which political prisoners convicted of even the most serious crimes were set free, while common criminals remained in prison for far less serious offenses. During 1977 and the early months of 1978, there were several spectacular breakouts and a large number of riots. Protestors destroyed many cell blocks, forcing the concentration of prisoners in the remaining facilities with increased overcrowding and the likelihood of further riots.

The government and the liberal press attempted to convince Spaniards that public order had not deteriorated significantly and that Spain was no harder hit by terrorism than many other countries. According to official statistics, however, between 1975 and 1976 the number of persons who lost their lives in "alterations of public order" jumped from 20 to 78, of whom 17 were policemen and 61 were civilians. According to press reports, during the 11 months following the June 1977 election, ETA alone killed 11 policemen and 13 civilians and wounded 67 other persons. If data were available on the activities of all left and right-wing terrorists, not merely of ETA, it would probably show that the incidence of terrorism in Spain was higher even than in Italy, although its concentration in the Basque country somewhat limited its impact on the rest of the country.

During 1977–78 there was considerable discontent, particularly among conservatives, with what appeared to be the government's inability to maintain order. Together with the economic crisis, violence and terror contributed to a sense of disenchantment with democracy that threatened to undermine support for the new institutions. Thirty-six percent of the respondents in a poll conducted in June 1978 considered that during the year since the election the political situation had deteriorated. Twenty-six percent said that things were about the same, leaving only 38 percent who thought things were improving politically. These attitudes reflected discontent with many things, not merely with disorder, but ongoing inability to guarantee order would certainly discredit democratic institutions.

CATALONIA: THE RETURN OF TARRADELLAS

The results of the elections elated Catalan nationalists. Despite the fears of some conservatives, the Catalans chose the path of negotiation with the government, backed by large but peaceful demonstrations, rather than violence or a unilateral declaration restoring the *Generalitat*.

The day following the election, Reventós saw both Suárez and Juan Carlos whom he pressed to permit the return of the exiled president of the *Generalitat*, Josep Tarradellas, and the formation of a Catalan assembly. Shortly thereafter, 62 of the 63 representatives and senators elected by the four Catalan provinces met in Barcelona as the Assembly of Catalan Representatives to demand restoration of the Autonomy Statute of 1932, freedom for all parties, total amnesty, and Tarradellas's speedy return.

The 78-year-old Josep Tarradellas had served for 23 years as president of the *Generalitat* in exile since his election by members of the Catalan parliament-in-exile in 1954. Tarradellas had been instrumental in the founding of the Second Republic in 1931 and had served as President of the Government of Catalonia during most of the Civil War. As president of the *Generalitat* in exile, however, Tarradellas focused his attention primarily on the recovery of Catalan autonomy, declaring that it was perfectly compatible with the monarchy.

Suárez was dismayed by the success of Socialists and Communists in Catalonia and anxious to gain the initiative in the region for more moderate groups. Contact with Tarradellas through a mutual friend had convinced him that the Catalan leader was a realist and a moderate with whom he could work. He astounded Spain on June 27, 1977 by meeting with Tarradellas in Madrid and arranging for him to see King Juan Carlos two days later. As a result of those meetings, the government agreed in principle to the restoration of the *Generalitat*, and Tarradellas recognized the monarchy and agreed to work within the existing legal framework.

Before the agreement could be implemented, many important details had to be worked out. During the preceding year, Tarradellas had quarreled frequently with other Catalan politicians who had attempted to negotiate with Suárez about Catalan autonomy. In his eyes, only the *Generalitat* represented Catalonia, and consequently only he or his delegates could deal with the government. He would have preferred to continue working alone to iron out the details of the *Generalitat's* restoration, but the pressure of public opinion made it essential to collaborate with the Assembly of Representatives. Negotiations during the summer were hampered by differences between the president of the *Generalitat* and the Assembly of Representatives. In the end, Tarradellas frequently ignored the representatives and went his own way.

On September 2, a government spokesman announced that a preliminary agreement had been reached. It was generally expected that the *Generalitat* would be restored by September 11 when Catalonia celebrated the *Diado*, its national day. Catalan members of the Cortes, however, were extremely dissatisfied with the agreement worked out by Tarradellas. It did not provide for the establishment of a Catalan parliament. On the other hand, it gave the power of appointing the president of the provisional *Generalitat* to the government rather than to the Assembly of Representatives, and foresaw the inclusion in the *Generalitat* of members of the provincial governments appointed by Franco. Suárez decided not to implement the agreement in the face of the Assembly of Representatives' sharp opposition.

More than a million people poured into the streets of Barcelona on September 11, 1977 to celebrate the *Diado*, although the *Generalitat* still had not been re-established. The Catalans were sure that it soon would be, and the mood was one of euphoria. Many realized that at first the *Generalitat* would have little authority, but they felt that even symbolic recognition of their aspirations augured well for real autonomy in the future.

Further contacts between Suárez and Catalan leaders in the Cortes convinced the President not to include Franco appointees in the *Generalitat*, but he continued to insist that for the moment there could be no Catalan parliament and that the president of the *Generalitat* would have to be appointed by the government.

THE BASQUE COUNTRY

The problems of the Basque country proved far more intractable than those of Catalonia. Separatist sentiment, of negligible importance in Catalonia, had strong supporters on the left in the Basque country, and some PNV leaders seemed to be leaning toward independence rather than autonomy. There was no Basque Tarradellas, no single leader with enough popular support to represent the Basques as he represented the Catalans. Furthermore, Basque exile leadership was unwilling to cooperate with the government, and the newly elected Basque members of the Cortes were more sharply divided among themselves over both goals and tactics than were their Catalan counterparts.

The greatest problem in the Basque country was the climate of violence. On June 22, 1977, police found the body of Javier de Ybarra, a prominent, wealthy industrialist, kidnapped and assassinated by the ETA after his family had refused to pay ransom. His assassination dispelled whatever hopes optimists may have had that the holding of elections would put an end to terrorism and kidnappings. Two months later the government attempted to obtain the extradition from France of Miguel Angel Apalategui, an ETA leader and a prime suspect in the assassination of Ybarra. Demonstrations and riots to protest the attempted extradition shook San Sebastián for six consecutive days. The fact that the government requesting the extradition was composed not of Franco appointees but of elected members of the Cortes did not weigh heavily enough to dispel widespread opposition to all police or judicial action against Basque nationalists. Moderate Basque leaders loudly condemned political violence when it occurred, but they continued to be unwilling to support governmental action against its authors.

Like their Catalan counterparts, the deputies and senators of the Basque provinces decided shortly after the election to form an Assembly of Basque Representatives. With the exception of the UCD members from Navarre, they met in Guernica on June 19 and issued a declaration calling for: total amnesty for all political prisoners; freedom for all political parties and labor unions; formation of interim caretaker city councils to take over from the Franco-appointed ones still in power; prompt municipal and provincial elections; recognition of Basque as an official language along with Castilian; and immediate administrative unification of the Basque provinces.

After the fanfare of its initial meeting, the Assembly of Basque Representatives accomplished little. The PNV and the PSOE who controlled it had demonstrated in the elections that they enjoyed far more support than the extremists, but during the summer they allowed the initiative to slip out of their hands. The extremists not represented in the Assembly organized the demonstrations in favor of Apalátegui and a six-week-long Basque freedom march by 3,500 people that ended in Pamplona with a rally of 75,000 people. In late August and early September the extra-parliamentary political groups organized an Amnesty Week which culminated on September 3 with a march of some 200,000 people in Bilbao. The PNV reluctantly decided at the last moment to co-sponsor this march which the PSOE refused to support. Despite this lack of enthusiasm on the part of the victors in the elections, it turned out to be the largest demonstration ever held in the Basque country. It was primarily an amnesty demonstration, but the far left took advantage of the opportunity to demand complete independence, voice support of ETA, and call for social revolution.

EMERGENCY ECONOMIC MEASURES

The composition of the new cabinet, and particularly the naming of Enrique Fuentes Quintana as Vice President for Economic Affairs, showed that after a year of neglect Suárez was finally turning his attention to Spain's economic problems. In the summer of 1977, the economy was suffering from three serious ills: a soaring deficit in the balance of payments; rising inflation; and high unemployment. In 1976, the deficit on current account had been $4.25 billion. During the first half of 1977 it had been about $2.3 billion, and economists were predicting it would reach $5 billion by the end of 1977. In 1976, the inflation rate had been 19 percent. During the first six months of 1977 the cost of living rose 13.2 percent and the pace was accelerating. During the month of July alone prices increased another 3.7 percent. Experts warned of more than 30 percent inflation for 1977 unless urgent remedies were applied. Unemployment, according to official figures, stood at five to six percent of the active population, but the trade unions and many private economists placed their estimates considerably higher.

Fuentes Quintana was especially concerned about the balance of payments problem. The first measure taken by the new economic team was a 19.6 percent devaluation of the peseta on July 12, 1977. Later in the month, the government announced a set of other economic measures. It urged moderation in salary increases, suggesting a target of 17 percent for the year. In return for the sacrifice implied in accepting salary increases significantly smaller than the anticipated increase in the cost of living, the government promised a thorough reform of Spain's archaic fiscal system to spread the burden of taxes more equitably. To guarantee that those who could afford to pay more actually did, it promised to modify the law to permit fiscal inspectors to investigate bank accounts, all of which had been protected by rigid secrecy since 1940. It also pledged to make more funds available for unemployment insurance and to give fiscal incentives for hiring new employees.

These proposals met with criticism both from the business community and from labor unions. Business leaders stressed the need for more incentives to invest and denounced the end of bank secrecy. Labor unions complained that the proposals placed almost all of the burden on the workers. They complained they were being asked to accept substantial losses of real wages in return for promises of future legislation that might never be implemented.

In August, the government proposed emergency economic legislation including tax cuts for businesses that took on new employees as well as a tax on wealth, an income tax surcharge, and luxury taxes. It hoped the new measures would bring in an additional $3 billion. Despite the sense of urgency the government had demonstrated in its statements, it took few other concrete measures during the rest of the summer, and even this minimal package of emergency measures was not finally approved until mid-November. Political commentators began to question whether Suárez had really grasped the critical urgency of the economic situation.

THE SEPTEMBER CRISIS

By mid-September the government's lack of initiative had dissipated all the enthusiasm generated by the June elections. Both politicians and the press began to question how much longer Suárez could hang on. He faced a deepening economic crisis, the hostility of bankers, business leaders, and labor unions, and growing dissension in the ranks of his own party. Pressure on the government was increased by the slowness of its negotiations in Catalonia and by its failure to restore order in the Basque country.

The key to success of the anti-inflation program was the cooperation of the working class. Suárez had met with union leaders in August and had proposed the formation of mixed commissions to discuss economic plans, but this was far from sufficient to guarantee their collaboration. Recent European experience had demonstrated how difficult a social pact was to obtain, even for a left-wing government. The prospects for success by Suárez's center-right UCD government, which had received only about a third of the popular vote in June, seemed bleak.

On both the left and the right, voices of alarm were raised. The leader of the Workers' Commissions, Marcelino Camacho, affirmed that "if a solution isn't found, we'll have a Pinochet." Basque industrialist Luis Olarra drew his analogy from Argentina: "If things continue like this, a Videla will come." Madrid was alive with talk of a government of national unity to take over from Suárez in this situation of general discontent and unrest.

The hastily assembled UCD coalition began to show its strains. One of its most prominent members, Fernando Alvarez de Miranda, President of the Congress of Deputies, called publicly for a government of national coalition. A steady stream of rumors about internal dissension led to insistent talk of breakup of the party. On September 28, the Minister for Parliamentary Relations, Ignacio Camuñas, resigned over differences with Suárez about the UCD's future organization. His resignation did not have any serious aftermath, but was indicative of the party's internal difficulties.

The government seemed unable to control the streets, as violence flared up in various parts of the country. In Barcelona right-wing radicals bombed the offices of a satirical left-wing paper. The explosion killed one person and injured ten. In Madrid, the funeral of a police captain shot to death by leftist radicals provided the occasion for anti-government demonstrations by the right.

In the midst of this tense atmosphere, the PSOE called for the resignation of the Minister of the Interior as a result of police man-handling of a Socialist deputy during a demonstration. Although the motion, which received no support from other parties, was doomed to failure, the Socialists insisted on a full-scale debate in the Cortes. Three months after being elected, the new Spanish legislature was forced to dedicate its first major debate to a lamentable incident of relatively minor importance compared to the great issues facing the country. The futility of the debate and its final outcome—decided by the votes of the UCD against the PSOE with all other groups abstaining—did nothing to enhance the prestige of the new democratic Cortes.

If the PSOE had wanted to enter the government, the atmosphere of discontent and paralysis that pervaded Spain in early fall might have led to the formation of a broad coalition government of national salvation. The Socialists, however, were still unwilling to consider such an alternative, either because they hoped that in the near future they might be able to form a government of their own, or simply because they did not want to accept responsibility at a difficult moment when no reliable solutions to the country's problems were in sight.

The Socialists, as well as the Communists and the representatives of the Catalan and Basque parties, were anxious to safeguard Spain's fragile new democratic institutions. They realized that, for the moment at least, the future of Spain was in Suárez's hands and that it was in their own long-term interest to help him overcome the crisis. Suárez, for his part, finally decided that he could afford no further delays and that he would have to make concessions to obtain the opposition's help. These attitudes made possible a sudden turnaround in the political environment between the end of September and the middle of October.

TOWARD CATALAN AND BASQUE AUTONOMY AND AMNESTY

Despite lingering opposition from the Assembly of Catalan Representatives to some details of his plan, on September 29 Suárez was able to announce the re-establishment of the *Generalitat*. The restored Catalan government was of much more symbolic than real importance. For the moment it had no power and its prospects of obtaining significant authority before approval of the Constitution were small. Still, its restoration signified recognition of the distinctive political character of the region and awareness of Catalan demands for autonomy.

Suárez installed Tarradellas as President of the *Generalitat* on October 24. Cheers and cries of "We want the [autonomy] statute [of 1932]!" greeted the new president. He responded, "Me, too," but was obviously pleased with what he had obtained and willing to wait until after approval of the Constitution for definitive autonomy measures. Most Catalans also seemed to realize that during the upcoming months they would do well to concentrate on the framing of the Constitution which would set the ground rules for the future status of the region.

Suárez's move in securing Tarradellas's collaboration and in restoring the *Generalitat* was eminently successful in channeling the energies of Catalan nationalists into constructive channels and avoiding potentially disruptive conflict. Catalans spoke ironically of their "decaffeinated" *Generalitat*, but the government's willingness to make even this symbolic concession convinced them real progress could be obtained through legal channels. There was some grumbling about the slowness with which functions were transferred to the *Generalitat*, and considerable animosity between its president and its Socialist members, but after restoration of the *Generalitat*, Catalan politicans generally concentrated on constitutional issues and saved their demands for a broader autonomy statute until after the Constitution had been approved.

In an effort to regain the initiative in the Basque country, the government and the Assembly of Basque Representatives began negotiating in September a pre-autonomy statute. Two serious problems immediately appeared. The representatives demanded fiscal autonomy and the inclusion of Navarre in the Basque region; the government was reluctant to grant the latter and bitterly opposed to the former.

While the Basque pre-autonomy statute was being negotiated, the government and the parliamentary opposition were working out the text of a new amnesty law which affected the whole country but principally interested the Basques. On October 8, 1977, they made public a draft which provided for total amnesty for all political crimes committed prior to the June 15 election, except those "carried out for profit or with the deliberate aim of destabilizing the democratic process begun December 14, 1976." The wording insured that the amnesty would benefit Basque nationalists but not GRAPO members nor militants of extreme right organizations.

Amnesty demonstrated the interplay of a moderately reformist conservative government, aroused public opinion, and an army hostile to liberalization. Had the government liberated in July 1976 all the prisoners it eventually set free, it would have met with stiff opposition from the extreme right and from the army. Military opposition to sweeping pardons was disarmed by the gradual nature of the process, and by the steps taken over the course of the intervening months to guarantee military discipline. On the other hand, without strong continuous pressure, a conservative government like Suárez's would never have gone as far as it eventually did.

Preparation of the amnesty led to some easing of tension in the Basque country even prior to the publication of the draft. On the day the draft was published, the military branch of ETA killed the president of the provincial council of Vizcaya and his two bodyguards in Guernica. Even the political-military branch of ETA condemned this assassination, but it was effective in demonstrating the extremists' refusal to be pacified by reform measures. For once the government responded energetically, striking both the right and the left. On October 10, the police announced the arrest of 17 members of GRAPO and of 13 neo-Fascists believed to have been involved in a recent bombing in Barcelona. This show of energy helped restore some public confidence in the government.

THE MONCLOA PACT

On October 5, 1977, Suárez asked the leaders of all the main political parties to join him in the Moncloa Palace for a two-day meeting to draw up an "emergency plan" for solving the "grave difficulties" facing Spain. In his invitation, he said "the delicacy of the moment and need to consolidate Spain's democracy have made it necessary to reach agreement between the political parties on how to solve some of the nation's basic political, economic and social problems." Reactions to the proposal varied, but no one refused the invitation to meet. After 20 hours of debate, on October 9 the leaders announced that they had reached a consensus on the broad outlines of an economic policy and of a program of political reform. By October 21, they had completed a 40-page text, which was signed on the 25th.

The economic part of the Moncloa Pact was essentially an austerity plan that offered social reforms and more parliamentary control over the economy in exchange for wage restraint. The government and the parties agreed to raise pensions 30 percent, increase unemployment benefits to the same level as the legal minimum wage, substitute progressive income taxes for indirect taxes, and undertake other fiscal reforms including new corporate taxes and a permanent tax on wealth. They pledged the creation of new classrooms for 700,000 more students in the public school system as part of a move toward completely gratuitous education. In addition, they promised to introduce the distinctive languages and cultures of the various regions into the school curriculum. Programs of slum removal, control of urban land speculation, and construction of subsidized housing would be undertaken to help alleviate the housing shortage. Both the social security system, whose budget was larger than that of the rest of the state administration, and government expenditures would be brought under closer parliamentary scrutiny and control. The pact also sketched out the basic principles of an agrarian reform program designed to convert renters into landowners and to put an end to share-cropping.

In return for these reforms, workers were asked to accept a ceiling of 22 percent on wage increases in 1978. This would represent stagnation of real wages, but not their decline since monetary and fiscal policy would be designed to keep inflation at or below 22 percent. Government expenditures and outlays of the social security system would increase no more than 21.4 percent, and growth of the money supply would be held to about 17 percent.

To guarantee that unions and private businesses would respect the 22 percent limit on wage increases, the pact stipulated that companies exceeding the limit by their own volition be penalized by withdrawal of fiscal exemptions and of government credits. If unions imposed raises greater than those permitted, management would be permitted to reduce by five percent the size of the work force.

The influence of Communists and Socialists on the Moncloa Pact was evident in the fixing of the wage ceiling at the same level as expected inflation, rather than well below it, as Fuentes Quintana had proposed to do. Many of the proposals for future reform legislation also reflected their demands. These were small gains, however, in comparison to the price labor was asked to pay. The willingness of the left-wing parties and the labor unions to accept the wage ceiling is a remarkable tribute to the maturity of the Spanish working class and to its sincere desire to contribute to the consolidation of democracy.

The Moncloa Pact contained in addition to the economic reform plan a political agreement about short-term legislative measures "to adapt the law to the demands of the new democratic reality" of Spain. The measures involved covered a broad range of topics. During the following months, much of this legislation was passed or at least introduced in the Cortes.

Control of television was entrusted to a council whose members were appointed by the government and the Cortes. The opposition continued to complain that the news was slanted in the government's favor, and in March 1978, the PSOE withdrew from the council in protest. The principle of parliamentary control has, however, been introduced, and if the political system continues to evolve toward democracy, television will certainly cease to be an instrument of government propaganda. Radio stations, which formerly were allowed to broadcast only news programs distributed by the government-controlled National Radio, were authorized to prepare their own news. New legislation also liberalized the control of political parties and removed some of the restrictions on them.

The government presented some legislation for reforming the police. The implementation of those proposals ought to make the police somewhat more efficient and responsive to the government's orders, but the reforms do not greatly change the basic structures. Responsibility for public order and crime prevention is still to be shared among the Civil Guard, a renamed Armed Police, and the General Police Corps. The Civil Guard is placed under the Ministry of the Interior rather than the army. The Armed Police, however, though renamed the National Guard, remain a militarized unit. Other bills attempt to make torturing prisoners a criminal offense, give arrested persons the right to consult a lawyer immediately, and strengthen the government's hand in dealing with terrorism without falling back on the draconian measures characteristic of the Franco regime.

Whatever structural changes are made in the police, law and order is still and will be for the foreseeable future in the hands of the same people who were responsible for it under Franco. A reformist government like Suárez's can change a few top commanders who get out of line, but it can do very little about the vast majority of the officers and men it has inherited from the past. Even if it were technically feasible to find replacements for them, it would not be politically practical.

The most important provision of the political pacts still to be acted upon is the revision of the code of military justice for the purpose of limiting the jurisdiction of the military courts and providing greater procedural guarantees to defendants. Despite the uproar caused when a military court in Barcelona sentenced a group of civilian actors to jail for having insulted the army, the government has been slow to move in this area.

The mentality of the Franco era still lingered on to a degree in some of the reform proposals included in the Moncloa Pact. Although in more limited fashion than before, they granted the government, for instance, the right to impose preventive detention on professional criminals. The right of assembly was restricted by the obligation to inform the police before holding even indoor meetings of more than 50 people, and all outdoor meetings required authorization of the police. Despite such limitations, however, the package of political reforms was an impressive one. The measures we have just mentioned, taken together with the reform of municipal elections and the new laws on labor unions foreseen in the Moncloa Pact, constitute a major step toward a free society.

MUNICIPAL ELECTIONS AND TRADE UNIONS

The Moncloa Pact temporarily created a consensus on economic policy, but other areas of conflict remained. In addition to the regional question, two of the most important were reform of local political life and restructuring the labor movement.

The dramatic changes taking place in Spanish political life at the national level in 1977–78 were not reflected at the local level. In some cities in the Basque country, new municipal councils were formed, but elsewhere almost all city governments remained in the hands of the councils and mayors appointed during the final years of the Franco regime. The government proclaimed repeatedly its belief that democracy must rest on a foundation of free, democratic municipal governments, and in July 1977, Suárez promised to hold municipal elections before January 1, but he reneged on that promise. In the face of strong pressure from the PSOE and other opposition parties, he relied on the votes of the AP to defeat attempts to force him to call elections promptly.

The reason for Suárez's reluctance to hold municipal elections is not hard to find. Even on the basis of the returns in the June 1977 national elections, it seemed likely that Socialists would control the city governments in the majority of Spain's large cities. Post-electoral polls showed the Socialists gaining strength steadily at the expense of the UCD. The President could not put off municipal elections forever, but it is understandable that he wanted to postpone them as long as possible in the hope that the UCD would regain some of the ground it had lost. Finally, he promised to call them within 30 days of the constitutional referendum. According to the law, the elections will be held 65 days after they are called.

The new municipal elections law worked out between the UCD and the PSOE was clearly designed to favor their interests as the two largest parties. Parties are required to present closed lists of candidates, making it very difficult for independents to even get on the ballot. Electoral alliances are allowed only for entire provinces, not for single towns or groups of towns. A particular coalition of small groups might successfully challenge the large parties in a given town, but such coalitions are much less likely to get on the ballot if they are required to take the same form in the entire province. These and other provisions of the law were designed to guarantee that either the UCD or the PSOE would win the municipal elections in most towns outside the Basque country and Catalonia where regional parties are powerful opponents. For some time to come, local political life in Spain is likely to remain less democratic than national political life.

Many of the considerations that influenced Suárez's thinking about elections also conditioned his approach to restructuring the labor unions. The "vertical syndicates" were finally disbanded by decree in September 1977. Except for their 34,000 employees, who were transferred to other government departments, no one mourned their passing. As we have seen, they had ceased to function long ago, but while they retained legal existence they were an impediment to the reorganization of Spanish labor.

With the vertical syndicates finally gone, election of labor representatives at the plant level became an urgent necessity; but there was no consensus among Spanish labor leaders on how the election should be run. Workers' Commissions had been active for years in the factories, and could present candidates who were well known and enjoyed local prestige. They wanted workers to vote for the candidates of their choice, drawn from an "open list" of candidates proposed by the various unions or running as independents. The Socialist union, UGT, had been much less active than the Workers' Commissions during the Franco years and had far fewer locally attractive candidates. On the other hand, it enjoyed organizational prestige among workers because of its historic traditions and its close ties to the European labor movement. It argued that each union ought to present its own slate or "closed list" and that the workers ought to choose a slate, without being able to pick some candidates from one and some from another.

The government favored the Communist proposal for several reasons. It would have liked to have a third large union, either totally independent of all parties, or affiliated with the UCD. Even the most optimistic, however, realized that over the short run there was no hope of putting together a whole new national union. A system of open lists that permitted locally prestigious moderates to win positions as independents was the best that the UCD could hope for.

Suárez may also have thought that a victory of the Communists would be preferable to one of the Socialist UGT. Since the Workers' Commissions were well ahead of the UGT in their organizational drive, they could afford to be less strident in their demands. They unequivocally supported the Moncloa Pact, whereas the UGT at first openly opposed it and then adopted an ambiguous position with regard to it. Suárez's business supporters were finding the Commissions easier to negotiate with and more responsible than the UGT, since the Commissions were better organized and more capable of guaranteeing that the workers would respect agreements they signed. Politically, Suárez was far more concerned about the PSOE than about the PCE. The former appeared to have a good chance of replacing the UCD as the government party in the next elections, and Suárez had no desire to strengthen its position by helping the growth of the UGT.

The government could ill afford to seem to take sides for the Workers' Commissions, especially when the Moncloa Pact was just being implemented, and it badly needed the PSOE's support. It adopted a compromise position, stipulating that closed lists would be used in all businesses with fewer than 250 employees; open ones were to be used in those with more than 250.

Union elections were held during the first semester of 1978. Published data on the results are not accurate. The figures given by the Ministry of Labor differ significantly from those put out by the news agency EFE. It is clear, however, that the Socialist Party failed to duplicate in the union elections its success in the legislative elections despite personal appearances by Felipe González and other party leaders. The Workers' Commissions certainly won the elections, although the margin of their victory is not clear. Between 35 and 40 percent of the men elected belonged to the Commissions. The UGT accounted for between 22 and 31 percent of the representatives, depending on the source consulted. Independents made a respectable showing, with roughly 12 percent of the candidates elected. Regional unions did very well in the Basque provinces, where they split the vote more or less evenly with the Commissions and the UGT. In Catalonia, however, regional unions failed miserably. The Commissions clearly dominate Catalonia, where they won more than 40 percent of the posts.

While the union elections were being held, new labor legislation was being drafted. Preparing new labor laws proved very difficult and gave rise to serious conflict. The government's project considered the union the sole bargaining agent of the employees, but provided for open shops. It offered the unions no voice in the operation of the business. The Cortes subcommittee that studied the bill was dominated by Socialists and Communists. They left the open shop provisions, but vastly increased union power. By the time they had finished amending it, the bill proposed an advanced form of co-determination.

This proposal for union participation on all levels of business decision-making provoked an outcry from the Spanish business community. The powerful Spanish Confederation of Business Organizations (CEOE) spoke ominously about "the social and economic ruin of the entire country." If the law passed as it had come out of the subcommittee, it threatened, there would be "no jobs, no salaries, no investment." The unions, for their part, rallied in defense of the project with threats of general strikes and a "French May" if it were watered down.

In the full Labor Committee, the UCD and its allies outweighed the PSOE and the PCE. When it emerged from the committee the bill once again looked very similar to the original UCD proposal. Unions would be able to participate in decision-making with respect to recreational facilities, company clinics, and the like (*obras sociales*), but not with respect to business decisions, where they were given a right to be informed but nothing approaching co-determination.

If labor had failed at least for the moment to win a voice in the management of businesses, it seemed to be defending quite successfully one of the most cherished rights it had acquired during the Franco period: almost absolute job security. The government's announcement that it was considering legislation to allow greater "flexibility in the work force," provoked a howl of protest from the unions that stopped the entire project. In order to preserve the atmosphere of compromise necessary to finish work on the constitution, the government decided to postpone for the duration legislative action on collective bargaining and other areas of labor-management relations.

REGIONALISM

By late November 1977, the Basque Assembly of Representatives had reached agreement with the government on the draft of a pre-autonomy statute that included only a vague reference to the desirability of future fiscal autonomy but foresaw the incorporation of Navarre into the Basque region together with Alava, Guipúzcoa, and Pamplona. This led to a new series of difficulties. According to a poll whose results were published at the end of November, only 20 percent of those interviewed in Navarre wanted to join a Basque region. Forty-seven percent were opposed and 33 percent undecided.

On December 3, 1977, Navarrese opposed to a Basque connection staged a demonstration in Pamplona. The senator who won the largest number of votes in Navarre, Jaime Ignacio del Burgo, a member of the

UCD, bitterly denounced the government's decision to sacrifice Navarre's autonomy to Basque ambitions. Partisans of inclusion of Navarre in the Basque region organized counter-demonstrations in Pamplona. The PSOE and the PNV threatened to hold massive public demonstrations and ETA warned of renewed violence if Navarre was not included in the Basque region. UCD members from Navarre pressured the government to respect their province's autonomy. Caught betweens these two forces, Suárez managed at the end of December to bring the two parties together to negotiate a compromise. The final agreement provided that Navarre would remain outside the Basque region until after new municipal elections. Then "an appropriate representative body" of the province will rule on the question. If its decision is favorable, as partisans of a Basque Navarre expect it to be, it will be submitted to a referendum, which defenders of an autonomous Navarre outside the Basque region are sure they will win.

This compromise permitted the government to announce on December 31 a pre-autonomy statute for a Basque region comprising Vizcaya, Guipúzcoa, and Alava, and in the future, possibly, Navarre. After a bitter dispute between the PSOE and PNV over how many representatives each would have, a Basque Council was formed with five members each of the PSOE and the PNV, three of the UCD, one of the EE, and one independent. It was expected to function in collegial fashion, with a largely honorary president.

Like the Catalan *Generalitat*, the Basque Council was of primarily symbolic importance and had no real authority. Nonetheless, the PSOE and the PNV quarreled violently again over the presidency. The PNV proposed Juan Ajuriaguerra, the Socialists nominated Ramón Rubial, national president of the PSOE and vice president of the Senate. The decision was up to the UCD, which eventually supported the Socialist candidate, a metal worker born in Vizcaya in 1906. Unlike Ajuriaguerra, but like the majority of his fellow countrymen, the new Basque president is unable to speak Basque. The PNV bitterly accused the UCD of having sold out to the PSOE in the Basque country to foster collaboration between the two parties on a national level.

Pre-autonomy and the formation of a Basque Council did little to pacify the region. Unlike the Catalans, the Basques were not willing to take these admittedly symbolic gestures as a pledge of real autonomy after the Constitution was approved. Marches, demonstrations, and violence continued to mark the rhythm of life in the region. Amnesty was no longer the burning issue it had been, but during the spring of 1978, violence flared up over the construction of a nuclear power plant at Lemóniz near Bilbao.

The Basque region has few energy resources, and produces only about 30 percent of its electricity needs. The two-million kilowatt nuclear plant at Lemóniz would help cover this deficit. Like nuclear installations in other parts of the world, it has drawn the protests of environmentalists and others concerned about the risks its operation entails. The Basque left has backed these protests, and some leftist Basque nationalists have described the construction of the nuclear facility as part of a genocide campaign.

The first large demonstration against Lemóniz took place in August 1976. In December 1977 ETA commandos attacked its Civil Guard post. Throughout the month of February 1978, they bombed and threw Molotov cocktails at the offices of the electric company responsible for the project and the homes and automobiles of its officials. In the midst of this wave of violence, the PNV proposed halting construction until a referendum could be held. The Basque Council requested that deliveries of uranium be held off until it had had time to study the question. A large anti-nuclear demonstration was held on March 13, 1978. Four days later the explosion of an ETA bomb in one of the generator rooms killed two workers, injured others, and caused extensive damage to the plant. Subsequently the Lemóniz issue slipped back into the background as ETA shifted its attention to other targets.

On the Basque national day, March 26, about a half million people demonstrated throughout the region. The celebration was relatively peaceful and no serious injuries were recorded. It is significant, however, that all parties except the UCD and the AP signed a proclamation describing inclusion of Navarre and recognition of Basque *sovereignty* as essential preconditions to the pacification of the region. The PNV had generally not used the term sovereignty in its declarations and the national PSOE sharply opposed the use of the term in reference to any region. This growing radicalization of Basque demands was reflected in the summer of 1978 during the debates on the Constitution, which we shall discuss in the next chapter.

The economic crisis all of Spain was suffering was aggravated in the Basque country by political unrest. Frequent strikes and demonstrations disrupted production. Businessmen faced with threats of kidnapping or subject to ETA's "revolutionary tax" began to close their plants or move them to other parts of Spain. Bankruptcies forced the closing of many smaller plants and by early 1978 began to affect the industrial giants like Babcock-Wilcox of Bilbao. As a result, unemployment in the Basque provinces was significantly higher than the national average.

Until the fall of 1977, regionalism seemed important only in Catalonia and the Basque country. The Canary Islands, Galicia, Valencia, and the Balearic Islands had historically shown some interest in regional autonomy and had small autonomy movements, but their specifically regional parties had failed to win a significant percent of the local vote in the June 1977 elections. Since the PSOE defended a federal system and the UCD professed to favor regional autonomy, their election victory in these four areas cannot be construed as a rejection of regional aspirations, but the weakness of regional parties does indicate that autonomy was not a pressing issue. In the rest of Spain there had been almost no indication of any interest in regional autonomy.

Progress toward autonomy in Catalonia and the Basque country soon stirred popular demands for similar concessions both in areas with some historic tradition of regional identity and in others with no such tradition. In November 1977, half a million people participated in a demonstration in favor of Valencian autonomy. In Andalucía police gunfire took the life of one youth and led to massive protests in December as up to three million persons demonstrated for autonomy. The government temporarily forbade further pro-autonomy demonstrations, saying that they were unnecessary since it was already working on plans to grant autonomy. By the spring of 1978 the autonomy movement had spread even to Castile and León, the heart of the historic Spanish monarchy.

This sudden surge of popular enthusiasm for regional autonomy was fed by a belief that it would help solve the economic problems of the less developed regions. It is far' from clear that autonomy would in fact be economically beneficial to underdeveloped regions that badly need transfer payments from richer areas, but many of the most popular slogans in autonomy demonstrations in Andalucía reflected the conviction that it would: "Jobs, Yes; Unemployment, No!" "Businessmen, Bankers, Invest Your Money Here!"

Regionalism presented special challenges in the Canary Islands, located one hundred miles off the coast of Morocco. The islands were incorporated into Spain in 1478 and have long been administered as part of the national territory. They profited from Spain's tourist boom, but remained underdeveloped. Illiteracy rates there are about 50 percent higher than the national average, and per capita income about one fifth below the national average. Since the European recession began in 1973, the islands have experienced a severe economic crisis. In mid-1978, unemployment was running about 12 percent.

Several years ago a labor lawyer, Antonio Cubillo, founded the Popular Movement for the Self-Determination and Independence of the Canarian Archipelago (MPAIAC) which Algeria has backed. The Suárez government did not take the movement very seriously until it became clear that Algeria intended to use the Canary Islands in its quarrel with Spain over the former Spanish Sahara. Suárez flew to the islands in response to a proposed resolution of the Organization of African Unity defining the islands as African territories colonized by Spain. In June 1978, the government approved a $350 million investment program for the two provinces, whose combined population is 1.2 million inhabitants.

Once it broke the ice with the approval of the Catalan *Generalitat*, the government showed no hesitation in granting pre-autonomy to other regions. Indeed, it was anxious to do so to make its concessions to the Catalans and Basques seem less dramatic. It did not consider the issue a very serious one, and probably thought that the eventual autonomy most regions would receive would be merely a form of administrative decentralization. By June 1978, ten regions with almost three-fourths of the population of Spain had been given pre-autonomy statutes: Catalonia, the Basque country, the Canary Islands, Galicia, Aragon, Castile-León, the Balearic Islands, Valencia, Extremadura, and Andalucía. Asturias and Murcia were awaiting approval of statutes which would permit them to be single-province regions. The statute of Castile-La Mancha was still being negotiated, principally because of questions about the incorporation of Madrid into the region. The provinces of León, Santander, and Logroño were included in the statute of Castile-León but had not decided to join, and Navarre remained outside the Basque Council. (See Map 5.1.)

Map 5.1

Map of Regions and Provinces, June 1977

Source: Adapted from *El País* (Madrid), June 15, 1978.

Many of the newly created regions have neither the historical traditions, the distinctive culture, nor the economic strength that will provide the underpinnings of Catalan and Basque autonomy. Their commitment to autonomy is superficial. Only 15 percent of the population in Andalucía and 11 percent of the population in Galicia say they would back autonomy if it meant higher taxes. Galicia and the Canary Islands can, for different reasons, make a good case for autonomous institutions on the scale of those Catalonia and the Basque country will demand. Most of the other regions cannot. The framers of the Constitution have tried to defer facing this problem by establishing a system which will make it difficult for most regions to acquire significant functions in the next five years. It remains to be seen what the outcome will be.

ECONOMICS AFTER THE MONCLOA PACT

In the weeks immediately following the signing of the Moncloa Pact, it appeared that it might not be possible to hold the line on wages. Massive strikes by civil aviation and Ministry of Public Works employees seemed to indicate that the unions were unwilling or unable to make workers accept the guidelines. This impression, however, proved false. By and large the Pact has been respected, and wages have not risen significantly faster than prices.

Thanks to wage restraints and to the slowing of the rate of increase of the money supply, inflation decreased significantly. The December 1976 to December 1977 increase in the cost of living was 26.4 percent, but between September and December 1977, prices rose only 4.3 percent. In the first quarter of 1978, prices increased 3.8 percent, compared to 7.8 percent in the same three months of 1977. Inflation was still a serious problem, but it no longer appeared out of control as it did during the summer of 1977.

The devaluation of the peseta in July 1977 together with the monetary and wage restraints imposed in the fall helped to boost Spanish exports and reduce imports and the commercial deficit. During the first quarter of 1978, imports were only 17.9 percent greater than during the corresponding period of 1977, but exports increased 42.8 percent. The commercial deficit decreased by 17.6 percent. The balance of payments position improved in even more spectacular fashion. In the first five months of 1977 the deficit had been $2.5 billion. In the first five months of 1978 it was only $197 million.

The slowing of inflation and the improvement in the balance of payments was due primarily to the austerity program, not to an upturn in economic activity. Spanish businessmen had not yet digested fully the double set of changes they faced simultaneously. As in the rest of the industrialized world, they had had to adjust to a much less favorable economic climate since oil prices began to rise. In addition, they faced a dramatic change in the conditions of the labor market as a result of the country's political transformation. The *sindicatos* had ceased to control labor years before Franco's death, and businessmen had learned to deal with the Workers' Commissions, but within a political framework that gave them certain assurances and limited the options of the illegal labor unions. Suddenly the labor unions enjoyed full legal status, the right to strike, and political support from the PSOE and the PCE that held almost 40 percent of the seats in the Cortes. The unions showed considerable moderation and sense of responsibility, but the business community was frightened by their Marxist ideology. Investments were already low because of the uncertain world economic outlook and because high salaries and low productivity had reduced profit margins. The new element of uncertainty introduced by the changes in the labor market led to a further drop in investment.

The export sector was the only part of the economy to experience much growth after the Moncloa Pact. Internal demand dropped; inventories grew; and in most sectors, production declined. At the end of 1977 industry was operating at 82 percent of capacity. In early 1978 utilization dropped to 80 percent. Under these circumstances, unemployment could only increase. According to the National Statistical Institute, in December 1977 there were 831,800 unemployed in Spain, amounting to 6.3 percent of the active population. During the first quarter of 1978 the number of unemployed went up another 100,000, to almost the one million mark which represented seven percent of the active population. In May 1978, unemployment was 57 percent greater than in May 1977. Sixty percent of the unemployed were under 25 and over 40 percent had never had a job. The high proportion of young people among the unemployed was due in part to legal obstacles to firing workers on the regular payroll, although as bankruptcies multiplied, they brought increasing unemployment even to workers whose positions had seemed secure.

The Suárez government faced a new crisis in February and March 1978. Economic conditions were becoming so difficult that even the largest concerns were finding it hard to stay afloat. The two largest steel makers in Spain were on the verge of bankruptcy. SEAT, the country's largest producer of automobiles, had alarmingly large inventories and was requesting permission to reduce the work week. Bilbao's giant Babcock-Wilcox filed for bankruptcy, and the medium-sized Bank of Navarre found itself unable to meet its obligations.

Business opposition to government economic policies, heightened by concern over Socialist and Communist sponsored proposals for worker participation in management decisions, found expression in a vigorous propaganda campaign conducted by the Spanish Confederation of Business Organizations. Despite its conservative political composition, the Suárez government had clearly lost much of the confidence of the business and financial community.

The workers were no more pleased with the government's performance than business. Implementation of measures against unemployment had been slow and the few measures that had been taken were proving entirely insufficient. The workers believed that they were being asked to bear in the form of unemployment too large a portion of the costs of stemming inflation. At the end of February 1978, Santiago Carillo, who had been one of the Moncloa Pact's most enthusiastic supporters, declared that it was virtually dead.

Even within the government, Fuentes found his support ebbing away. Suárez took an interest in the economy only when problems threatened his political plans; at other times he preferred to concentrate on the political problems which he understood better, leaving economics to his subordinates. Since Suárez was the only real source of power and authority in the government, this meant that the economy generally got little attention. Fuentes's position as Vice President for Economic Affairs gave him no real authority over heads of the other economic ministries who often flatly rejected his plans or failed to cooperate in putting them into effect.

On February 24, 1978, Fuentes resigned. The mechanisms of his resignation are not entirely clear. In statements after the fact, he suggested that he had done all that a technician could do, and what was now needed was a politician who could implement the measures he had designed. It seems that Fuentes's frustration with his inability to obtain cooperation and support, rather than a desire on Suárez's part to change policy, did in fact lie at the root of the resignation.

Suárez, in any case, took advantage of the resignation to rearrange his economic team. He named no new Vice President for Economic Affairs. Instead, the Vice President for Political Affairs, Fernando Abril Matorell, added to his duties those of Minister of Economics. Fernández Ordóñez remained at Finance, and the Ministers of Commerce and Public Works also retained their positions, but the Ministers of Industry, Agriculture, Labor, and Transportation were all replaced. The most significant change was the appointment of Augustín Rodríguez de Sahagun, former Vice President of the Confederation of Spanish Business Organizations (CEOE) as Minister of Industry. While working for the CEOE, he had organized many of the campaigns against the government's economic policy, and especially against the Socialist/Communist proposal for worker participation in management. The new shape of the cabinet did not suggest a sharp change in government policy but did increase the influence of business interests.

MARCH MINI-CRISIS

The cabinet reorganization contributed to a new crisis in the relations between the UCD and the PSOE. The Socialists, who were already discontented with Fuentes's policies, were appalled by what appeared to them to be a shift further to the right. In the political sphere, the PSOE deeply resented the government's breaking its promise of holding municipal elections in 1977 and its use of the votes of the AP to postpone them until after the constitutional referendum. The PSOE also complained that the reorganization of the state-owned television had been a sham which had not given the opposition a real voice in its operations. For months Socialists and Centrists had collaborated effectively, and at times even cordially, in the preparation of a draft of the Constitution. Now, however, they quarreled violently over the constitutional provisions about education. The UCD wanted to guarantee the position of private and Catholic schools, while the PSOE wanted to strengthen the public schools at their expense.

To register his party's discontent over the constitutional issue and the general political situation, on March 7, 1978, the PSOE member withdrew from the subcommittee drafting the Constitution. The subcommittee's work was almost finished, but the withdrawal signified a serious breakdown in the consensus that Spain needed both to finish the Constitution and to master the different economic situation.

The left and right combined to demand an explanation from the government of the February ministerial crisis. Their decision to reject a spokesman's initial explanation as inadequate forced Suárez to speak to the Cortes. The President knew that the Socialists had no real desire to provoke a serious crisis at this time and that he still effectively controlled the situation. In his statement to the Cortes, he added little to the explanations already given about the reasons for the crisis, but reaffirmed his desire for consensus and a working understanding with all parties. He argued that approval of the Constitution must take precedence over all other matters, and presented his government as largely a caretaker. Real political life, he suggested, could only begin once the Constitutional Referendum had been approved.

While not deceived by Suárez's claims about the nonpolitical character of his administration, the opposition fundamentally agreed that the business of the Constitution was of overriding importance, and had no real desire to overthrow the government. The Socialists had already agreed to sign the draft of the Constitution, and they did not follow through on their threats of mass demonstrations to force prompt municipal elections. The idyllic atmosphere of the period immediately after the signing of the Moncloa Pact had been definitely lost, but the PSOE and the UCD continued to collaborate both in preparing the Constitution and in other less transcendental matters. Once again, as in the fall, the crisis dissipated without leaving serious scars. During the rest of 1978 the most important questions were those relating to the preparation of the Constitution, which we will discuss in the next chapter. As background for that subject, we will consider here the Basque question and its public-order aspects, as well as the economic situation.

THE BASQUE QUESTION AND PUBLIC ORDER

Our lengthy discussion of the Basque question in the preceding section should have made it clear that it can, in no way, be reduced to a simple problem of maintaining public order. In fact, its public-order aspects are secondary compared to the issues of collective identity and self-government it entails. These broader issues will be examined in the following chapter in the context of the constitutional debates. Here we will be concerned with the problem of public order in general, and especially in the Basque country.

The numerous demonstrations, acts of terrorism, and cases of police violence that agitated the Basque country during the spring and early summer of 1978 reached a peak in July as a result of frequent confrontations between groups favoring and opposing the incorporation of Navarre into the Basque region. On July 8, shortly before the feast of San Fermín (the patron of Navarre, in whose honor the bulls are run through the streets), pro- and anti-Basque demonstrators clashed in the bullring of Pamplona. This provoked an ill-advised action by the Armed Police, which touched off rioting first in the bullring and then in the central section of Pamplona; after the police fired live ammunition, which killed one youth, rioting in fact spread throughout the Basque contry. Protesters clashed frequently with the police and cut off the road from San Sebastián to France. For several days there was no rail or road traffic between France and the Basque country, and many stores and businesses were shut down. In the course of the demonstrations, another youth was killed. In the small town of Rentería the police went on a rampage, smashing shop windows, looting stores, and firing tear gas and smoke grenades at random.

At almost the same time as the crisis in the Basque country, leftist terrorists in Madrid, who may have been connected with the ETA, shot and killed Brig. Gen. Juan Sánchez Ramos and his aide. General Sánchez was
the highest-ranking officer to be killed since the assassination of Adm. Luis Carrero Blanco in December 1973.

A brief period of relative calm followed. The onset of summer heat traditionally brings political life to a virtual standstill in Spain, and in 1978 even ETA terrorists seemed to take a summer vacation that lasted through most of August.

At the end of August, four assassinations of law-enforcement officers in a single day—two in the Basque country, one in Catalonia, and one in Galicia—signaled the end of the respite. The Professional Police Association (APP) responded to the killings with a note whose main theme was: "We have had enough!" It criticized the government, the parties, and the trade unions for failing to support the police and thereby contributing to the violence that had cost the lives of 16 law-enforcement officers since the beginning of the year.

The APP note came at a time when the government was already under fire for its failure to control the police. Members of the Basque Council had charged that the police were tapping their phones, and insistent rumors were circulating that the police were also controlling the minister of interior's own phone. In September a political-scandal magazine published the text of intercepted phone conversations of leading politicians, and claimed that it had obtained the texts from illegal police wiretaps.

The government denied the charges of illegal wiretapping by the police, and opened proceedings against the officers of the Professional Police Association who had been responsible for the protest note. The APP, however, refused to back down, confirming the positions of its accused members and reiterating its support of the note. The Suárez government decided not to fight on this issue, accepting at face value the APP's statement that the original note was not intended to be disrespectful of the parties, nor of the unions. "The motive which led the Interior Ministry to take action against several members of the board of the APP," a government spokesman declared, "no longer exists."

ETA terrorists struck again repeatedly in October. On the fourth they assassinated Navy Captain Francisco Liesa, the executive officer of the Bilbao Naval District. On the thirteenth they killed two armed policemen in the outskirts of Bilbao, bringing to 23 the number of law-enforcement officers killed during the year, including seven in the space of three weeks.

During the funeral of their comrades on October 14, some 800 of the 2,000 members of the Armed Police assigned to Bilbao staged a demonstration and sit-in. They insulted the inspector of the Armed Police, the director general of security, and other officials attending the funeral. In an attempt to calm the irate police, the government arranged for most married members of the Armed Police to be transferred out of the Basque country, and expelled from the corps 25 protagonists in the incidents. The situation was so tense that the government decided to postpone a Cortes debate on public order originally scheduled for October 25.

In late October, many observers were encouraged by what they thought were signs of a shift in the attitude of the Basque Nationalist Party (PNV) toward ETA violence. PNV leaders had regularly condemned

ETA's assassinations, but often seemed, no many non-Basques, to be overly understanding of the assassins' motives. *El Pais*, a liberal Madrid daily, for example, on September 26 had charged the PNV with carrying on, consciously or otherwise, "a policy which in the final analysis gives moral support to the terrorists' actions." At the end of October, the PNV sponsored a march in Bilbao against violence; some 35,000 people filed silently through the capital of Vizcaya, while, not many blocks away, police fought with pro-ETA demonstrators. Moderate Basques and non-Basques alike hailed the antiviolence march as a sign of the PNV's long-awaited decision to speak out unequivocally against ETA. If their interpretation is correct, the march will go down in history as an important turning point, but at this writing (December 1978), it is still to early to say for sure whether the PNV has broken altogether with ETA.

The leaders of the PNV do not seem to have decided at this juncture what their maximum and minimum goals are for the medium and long range. They appear even less clear on what role they see ETA violence playing in the achievement of their own aims. Some doubts about their goals arise almost necessarily from their decision to encourage their followers to abstain in the referendum, and from their declarations about the right of secession. As regards means, the PNV did little during the tense, violence-filled weeks preceding the referendum to reaffirm its opposition to ETA terrorism. The march against terrorism was a dramatic gesture, but whether it was anything more than that remains to be seen.

The government responded to ETA violence with a 15-point plan for special measures, such as more intense patrolling, establishing of roadblocks, and searching of pedestrians and drivers, but stopping short of suspending guarantees of personal freedom. The PNV criticized the government's plan as being like aspirin that lowers the patient's fever but does nothing to cure the disease. It put forward its own 15-point counterplan for the pacification of *Euzkadi*, which stressed political concessions as a prerequisite for peace. The government did agree on October 24 to study the formation of an autonomous police force in the Basque country, but this negotiating gambit is unlikely to produce any substantive results in the near future.

On November 10, most of the major political parties held marches throughout Spain to protest against terrorism. The UCD, the PSOE, and the unions wanted to demonstrate that the vast majority of the population opposed terrorism and disorder. Some 200,000 people demonstrated in Madrid and about another 130,000, in Barcelona; but the most significant fact was that no such marches took place in the Basque country, apparently because the national organizers feared that demonstrations would trigger new violence there.

Five days later the Civil Guard in Mondragón (Guipúzcoa) machine-gunned and killed three persons—two presumed ETA terrorists whom they had been pursuing, and a middle-aged bystander. The shots sparked a general strike in Guipúzcoa and a war of communiqués between the Basque Council and the Ministery of the Interior over the exact nature of the events. In the midst of this crisis, ETA terrorists in Madrid assassinated a Supreme Court justice who had previously been president of the Public Order Tribunal.

Under the strain of the increasing tempo of terrorist attacks, the discipline of the armed forces appeared to be cracking. In mid-November, word reached President Suárez of plans for a coup scheduled to be carried out on November 17 after King Juan Carlos's departure for Mexico. On the night of November 16, army investigators arrested Civil Guard Lt. Col. Antonio Tejero Molina and Armed Police Capt. Ricardo Sáenz de Inestrillas, thereby breaking up the plot. Government officials were concerned, however, that the roots of the aborted conspiracy might have run much more deeply into the army.

On the seventeenth, before any information about the plot had been made public, but when rumors were running wild through the upper levels of the armed forces, Defense Minister Gutiérrez Mellado was forced to arrest a regional commander of the Civil Guard for insulting him during a meeting with high-ranking officers. The arrested general, Juan Atares Peña, had commanded the Civil Guard in the Basque country until March 1978.

Neither of these incidents was in itself as serious as the disturbances among the Armed Police in the Basque country on October 14, but the government feared they were signs of dangerous unrest among officers. General Gutiérrez Mellado's reforms and transfers had removed most politically dangerous generals from sensitive positions, but many field-grade officers of questionable loyalty remained in key positions. It is impossible to generalize with any confidence about the attitudes of the Spanish army in the weeks preceding the referendum. The Constitution's concessions to Basque and Catalan regionalism, and the government's failure to restore order in the Basque country, seem, however, to have alienated the goodwill many officers had shown two years earlier and to have converted the neutrality of others into outright hostility toward liberalization.

Even taking these factors into account, governmental and public reaction to "Operation Galaxia," as the abortive plot was known, seems disproportionate to the seriousness of the threat. The government and the press may have chosen to give the incident considerable play in order to convince voters of the importance of taking part in the upcoming constitutional referendum; certainly, the news of the military plot did stimulate the campaign for a "yes" vote.

The third anniversary of Franco's death took place in the midst of this tense atmosphere. On November 20, rightist crowds, variously estimated at between 125,000 and 300,000, gathered in the Plaza de Oriente in Madrid to roar their disapproval of the Constitution and to denounce the "traitors" responsible for "dismembering Spain." Despite the size of the demonstration, it came off without incident, and this fact alone served to reduce tension during the following days.

In the Basque country, ETA violence continued to crescendo right up to the day of the referendum. During the month of November, ETA terrorists killed 15 persons and wounded 19 others. In addition, they planted numerous bombs; stopped, at gunpoint, a theater's film program in order to lecture the audience; and generally gave the impression of being able to operate at will. The police made many arrests but failed to control the violence. On the other hand, ETA did not succeed in forcing the government to suspend personal liberties or declare martial law. To this extent, despite its many successes, its campaign failed.

ECONOMIC CONDITIONS

After Fuentes Quintana's resignation and Abril Matorell's appointment, the Spanish economy continued to move within the fairly narrow limits already set for it, although two fortuitous events made its performance during 1978 better than it might have been. First, favorable weather conditions led to bumper harvests and to slightly lower agricultural prices, thereby lessening the inflationary pressure. In addition, tourist receipts rose by more than a third, to almost $5 billion, much strengthening the Spanish balance of payments.

During the first ten months of 1978, prices rose 14.2 percent. Though inflation was still a serious problem, this performance compared favorably with the 24.2 percent inflation rate during the same ten months of 1977. Government economists predicted that the year's inflation would be slightly lower than the 16 percent target set in the Moncloa Pacts.

Thanks to large tourist revenues, increasing foreign investments in Spain, falling imports and rising exports, and an improvement in the services account, Spain's balance of payments at the close of 1978 was favorable. During the first nine months of the year, imports exceeded exports by $2.9 billion, but the balance on the current account was positive by $1.6 billion, and the overall balance of payments showed a surplus of $3.6 billion. If the general level of economic activity picks up, Spain will be forced to increase sharply her imports of both raw materials and machinery, but for the moment the balance of payments presents no problems. At the end of October 1978, the country's reserves in gold and foreign currencies amounted to $9.6 billion, up from about $4 billion in June 1977.

Excellent harvests, a booming tourist industry, and growing foreign demand for Spanish products account for a 2.5–3 percent increase in gross internal product during 1978, when the Moncloa Pact called for only a 1 percent increase. This growth was largely confined to the foreign sector. Internal demand increased by only about 0.5 percent and gross internal capital formation declined by close to 3 percent. Growth in the primary sector of the economy was about 5 percent. Industrial production increased by a modest 2 percent, and construction declined by about 1.5 percent.

Unemployment continued to grow during the second half of 1978. According to the Bank of Spain's estimates, the number of unemployed increased by about 150,000 during the year, and total unemployment stood at close to 8 percent as the year came to an end. The situation was particularly serious in the southern agricultural provinces, where unemployment exceeded 10 percent. All parties agreed on the seriousness of the problem, but there was no consensus on its solution. Business leaders and government officials insisted that inflation must be further reduced to stimulate investment that would generate new jobs; on the other hand, the labor unions demanded large public investments and programs designed to create jobs.

The different approaches to the problem of unemployment were among the most important obstacles to negotiating a new economic agreement to replace the one-year Moncloa Pact; discussions of the subject began in August and a target date of September was set. A new agreement would have to be negotiated by the labor unions and business organizations rather than by the political parties that worked out the Moncloa Pact. The Communist-dominated Workers' Commissions enthusiastically supported the idea of a new pact and talked of impending catastrophe, if negotiations failed. But the Socialist UGT received the idea coldly and said that there would be no need for a policy of consensus after the referendum.

Abril Matorell showed little energy or enthusiasm in pushing forward with the negotiations. He held a discussion session with the unions in October but did not present concrete proposals until mid-November. By that time the Workers' Commissions had adopted a considerably tougher position, demanding 16 percent wage increases for the coming year, whereas the government was talking about a 12.5 percent ceiling on wages in order to reduce inflation to 10 percent. The government's plan called for creating 150,000 new jobs, but the Workers' Commissions pointed out that 200,000 young persons would be entering the labor force and called for at least 300,000 new jobs. The Communists also demanded that the political parties participate in the negotiating of any agreement between unions and business organizations so as to foster the structural reforms promised in the Moncloa Pact but never carried out. They especially insisted on democratization of publicly owned industries and worker participation in the running of the social security system.

As the referendum approached, no one appeared anxious to negotiate a sweeping new economic and social pact, at least until new elections were held, or until the formation of a new government with a solid majority in the Cortes clarified the political situation. As had happened repeatedly since Franco's death, political considerations pushed economic ones into the background.

6

THE CONSTITUTION

THE DRAFTING PROCESS

Writing the Constitution took a little over a year. For our purposes, there is no need to follow every step of the drafting and the negotiations that led to the final text. We shall outline briefly the process by which the Constitution was prepared and then examine its major provisions, discussing at the same time the principal controversies that arose.

The first draft was prepared by a subcommittee of the Congress of Deputies, the Committee on Constitutional Affairs. Three of its seven members belonged to the UCD. In addition, there was one Socialist, one Communist, one member of the Popular Alliance, and one representative of the regional parties. Had the last named been a Basque, the Basque deputies might have been more enthusastic about the drafting subcommittee's work, but the representative of the regional parties was in fact a Catalan.

If the UCD had been interested in forcing through its own proposals, it would in most cases have had little difficulty in picking up one vote from the AP, the regional delegation, or even the PCE. King Juan Carlos and President Suárez were determined, however, to obtain the widest possible consensus on the Constitution, and this absolutely required compromise with the Socialists. Suárez had repeatedly rejected the idea of forming a government of national unity, but just as the Moncloa Pact was the result of an understanding with the main opposition forces, so too the Constitution would be shaped in genuine consultation between the UCD, the PSOE, and the other opposition groups.

The subcommittee worked in closed session. After each meeting a brief communiqué gave the main outlines of the Articles approved, but the text itself remained rigorously secret until the entire first draft was completed in mid-November 1977. The subcommittee had agreed to continue working in secret until it had finished revising and was ready to make its report to the Committee on Constitutional Affairs, but a magazine got hold of a copy of the first draft and published the first thirty-nine articles. A few days later a Madrid daily published the entire text. This breach of confidentiality gave rise to a beneficial broad public debate in the early stages of the Constitution's formulation.

In mid-December the subcommittee finished revising the draft and presented it to the full committee. A comparison of the first and second drafts shows that the changes introduced were numerous and substantial, affecting such vital issues as the method of election of members of the Cortes, the role of the king in naming the President of the Government, and the structure and function of future autonomous regions.

The weeks after Christmas witnessed a vigorous political debate about the future Constitution that culminated in the presentation by individual members of the Cortes and party caucuses of over 1,100 proposed amendments to the second draft, which was then returned to the subcommittee for final revision.

At this point, the atmosphere of compromise which had enabled the members of the subcommittee to agree to a text despite sharp differences of opinion, appeared to be in real danger of breaking down. The PSOE and the UCD were bitterly opposed over constitutional provisions about the Church, about education, and about lockouts. While the final subcommittee revisions were being made, the UCD demanded some further changes in the articles on education which the PSOE considered already to be in final form. When the UCD insisted on pushing through its amendments, the Socialist member, Gregorio Peces-Barba, withdrew from the subcommittee in protest.

Seen in retrospect, the Socialist member's withdrawal appears to have been a tactical maneuver. By that time, the subcommittee had virtually finished its work. Peces-Barba's presence at its final sessions would not have permitted the Socialists to introduce further substantial changes in the text. His withdrawal was intended to convince the UCD that the Socialists were serious in their demands and that they would require substantial concessions as the price of their support of the Constitution. It also permitted the PSOE to criticize the draft and to tell its electorate that the features of the Constitution it did not like were inescapable impositions of the UCD. Peces-Barba and other Socialists immediately began to attack the draft, which they castigated as a project for one of the world's most reactionary constitutions. This maneuver appealed to the core constituency of the PSOE, but struck most other observers as ridiculous.

However, in the end, Peces-Barba agreed to sign the subcommittee's final report. With his return the atmosphere of compromise revived.

The text next went to the full 36-member Committee on Constitutional Affairs. The UCD, with 17 members, was only one short of an absolute majority in the committee, and held both the presidency and first vice-presidency. It had not nominated many of its most brilliant or best-known members for the committee, apparently preferring to reserve its big guns for the debate on the floor of the Congress of Deputies. By contrast, the 13 Socialist members included most of the party's leaders: Felipe González, Alfonso Guerra, Enrique Múgica, and Joan Reventós. The PCE was also represented by its outstanding leaders, Santiago Carillo and Jordi Solé Tura. AP's delegation would be dominated by Manuel Fraga Iribarne. The Catalans were represented by Miguel Roca, who had served on the subcommittee; the Basques by Xavier Arzallus of the PNV.

Debate in the full committee began on May 5, 1978. Among the most hotly debated issues were the ones that had provoked Peces-Barba's withdrawal from the subcommittee (the position of the Catholic Church, the use of lockouts by employers, and state aid to and control over private education), but the presence of a Basque representative also brought to the fore the question of regional autonomy. It would prove the most intractable of all.

The UCD and the PSOE had already arrived at a working agreement on most points during the course of previous discussions, but nonetheless, the early sessions went slowly. During the first six, only 24 articles were approved. As the committee approached the most polemic topics, it began to appear that the UCD and the PSOE might reach a complete falling out. To avoid that eventuality, President Suárez resorted once again to a private pact, this time worked out between the First Vice President for Political Affairs, Fernando Abril Matorell, and the Organizational Secretary of the PSOE, Alfonso Guerra. The agreement was reached in a Madrid restaurant at a dinner that went on until 4:00 A.M. on May 29. That afternoon, the committee gave its approval to 27 articles, including some of the ones over which the two parties' disagreements had been most sharp. The Basques and the AP protested against what they criticized as an anti-democratic procedure for imposing the will of the two large parties on the minorities without even giving them a chance to express their views, but their protests went unheard. During the following days, party representatives met in closed session in the mornings to work out an agreement on the articles to be voted on in the open session in the afternoon, when debate was kept to a minimum. By June 20, the committee had fully revised the text which was now ready to be debated on the floor of the Congress of Deputies.

The Congress of Deputies began its examination of the text on July 4. To accelerate the debates, the deputies set a 15-minute limit on speeches.

The UCD and the PSOE were anxious to move ahead as quickly as possible and to avoid acrimonious debates which might poison the atmosphere of consensus with which they hoped to surround the birth of the Constitution. Before debate began, they retracted all the amendments they had proposed that had not been accepted by the other side during the previous phases. Their control of the chamber and their firm determination to avoid a break guaranteed that a consensus would eventually be reached on even the most hotly disputed issues. The AP proposed 40 amendments designed to reduce the autonomy of the future regions and to favor private education. On the other hand, the Basques were determined to increase the autonomy of the regions.

The most serious difficulties arose over the question of regional autonomy. After long and laborious negotiations between the PNV and the UCD, the compromise was reached, but at the last moment the UCD withdrew the proposal on which it was based.

The final vote on the entire text of the Constitution, taken on July 21, was 258 "yes" votes, 2 "no" votes, and 14 abstentions. One of the "no" votes came from the far left (EE), and the other five from the far right. Twelve members of the AP and two members of the Catalan Republican Left abstained. A total of 76 deputies were absent when the vote was taken. The PNV deputies all refrained from attending the session, in protest against the Constitution's failure to guarantee the historic privileges of their region, and against its inadequate provisions for regional autonomy.

The Congress of Deputies sent the text of the Constitution to the Senate. Despite the presence of a large number of independents, including the 41 senators appointed by the king, the UCD and the PSOE controlled the upper chamber as firmly as they did the lower; so there was never any doubt that the Senate would eventually approve the main lines of the Constitution, worked out in the Congress of Deputies.

The Senate Committee on Constitutional Affairs met for the first time on August 9, 1978. Eleven of its 25 members belonged to the UCD, five to the PSOE, two to the Catalan group, one to the Basque group, and six to other groups. It employed slightly more than a week in classifying and arranging the 1,254 amendments offered by senators, and then began its substantive debate on August 18. The large number of amendments proposed was the first sign that passage in the Senate might take much more than the month that observers had been predicting for it.

Education was one of the most hotly debated issues in the Senate, just as it had been in the Congress of Deputies. Many UCD senators disliked the compromise reached in the lower house and tried to modify it in favor of private schools. Party discipline and pressure from the Socialists forced them to withdraw their numerous proposals of amendments to the article that dealt specifically with education; but they successfully defended the inclusion in another article of a pledge to interpret the Constitution's guarantees in the light of the 1948 Universal Decalaration of Human Rights, which stresses parents' rights in education.

Many senators were annoyed by what they considered the UCD members' heavy-handed attempts to modify the consensus on education reached in the lower house. Their irritation increased in mid-September when centrist senators forced through two further amendments to guarantee the central government's role in cultural and eductional affairs in the regions and to protect Navarre from being coerced into joining the Basque region. Largely as a result of their irritation, during the committee's final session on September 14, its members approved a Basque-sponsored amendment that pledged restoration of the historic privileges of the regions (*fueros*) without specifically stating that this would be done only within the framework of the Constitution's other provisions. The amendment also changed the procedure for negotiating the restoration, authorizing the government, rather than the Cortes, to deal with the regional governments.

Committee approval of the Basque amendment stunned the government and lent new urgency to the efforts that had been going on all summer to find a regional-autonomy formula acceptable to the UCD, the PSOE, the majority of Spaniards, and the army, as well as to the Basque nationalists. The government negotiated intensively with the Basque representatives on the one hand and the parliamentary groups on the other. As had happened in the Congress of Deputies, it failed to reach an agreement with the Basques but worked out an accord with the other groups, not on the floor of the Senate but over a restaurant table, during a supper meeting on September 28. Representatives of the UCD, the PSOE, and the Catalan Minority agreed to return to the wording designed by the lower house, which amounted to nothing more than an expression of goodwill with respect to the fueros.

The debates on the floor of the Senate between September 25 and October 5 were not particularly interesting, nor eventful, since all important issues were worked out between party leaders outside the Senate chamber. Unlike the Congress of Deputies, the Senate did not take a vote on the Constitution as a whole but limited itself to approving the separate articles.

The Constitution emerged from the Senate in a clearer and better-written verion than the draft prepared by the Congress of Deputies, but essentially unchanged. The revised text strengthened the ties between the Senate and the regions, but not enough to make the upper house a chamber of the regions. It provided for a slightly more powerful Senate by giving the upper chamber the right to initiate legislation and to establish its own investigating committees.

Between October 16 and October 25, a joint Senate-Congress of Deputies Commission composed of five members of the UCD, three members of the PSOE, one member of the PCE, one of the Catalan Minority, and one independent prepared a final draft of the Constitution. In addition to reconciling the differences between the two texts, it added a stipulation that within 30 days of the new Constitution's promulgation, the President must either call for new elections or seek a vote of confidence in the Congress of Deputies. This provision put an end to speculation that Suárez might attempt simply to stay on as president once the Constitution had been approved.

Both chambers took a final vote on the Constitution on October 31. With 345 of the 350 deputies present, 325 deputies, including all but one of the Catalans, voted "yes"; the far-left Basque deputy, Francisco Letamendía, and five members of the Popular Alliance voted "no"; and all seven PNV deputies, one UCD member from Navarre, three Popular Alliance members, and three other deputies abstained. In the Senate, 239 of the 248 senators were present for the vote, and 226 voted "yes"; there were five "no" votes, including that of one admiral, two Basques, and one Catalan; and five Basques, one Catalan, and two military men abstained. The only surprise in the voting was that none of the three military men in the Senate, all of whom had been named by Juan Carlos, voted for the Constitution.

THE CONSTITUTIONAL REFERENDUM

All major national political parties and the principal Catalan groups campaigned in favor of a "yes" in the referendum. Opposition to the Constitution was concentrated in the Basque country and, on the national level, on the far right and far left. The PNV urged its members to abstain, while the *abertzale* parties called for a "no" vote. On the far right, the Fuerza Nueva, the Falange Española, and the conservative Carlists rejected the Constitution. The Popular Alliance was split over the issue. Its main body, led by Fraga Iribarne, urged its followers to vote "yes," while the groups headed by Federico Silva Munóz and Gonzalo Fernández de la Mora called for a "no." On the far left, some groups, like the Communist Revolutionary League (LCR), campaigned for abstention or a "no" vote, while others, like the Workers Revolutionary Organization (ORT), called for a "yes."

The Catholic Bishops Conference voted on November 24 to ratify a commission report of September 28, which pointed out certain positive and negative aspects of the Constitution and concluded that there were no overwhelming religious or moral motives to urge Catholics to vote one way or the other. A few days later, the cardinal of Toledo made public a pastoral letter that stopped short of calling for a "no" vote, but emphasized the Constitution's shortcomings in the areas of education, family, etc. This pastoral letter, which was ratified by eight other bishops, provoked violent criticism from many partisans of the Constitution, especially among the Socialists.

Despite the upsurge of terrorism in the Basque country, the government successfully resisted pressure to declare martial law or otherwise limit citizens' civic rights during the referendum campaign. To avoid possible violence, on November 23 it did prohibit all outdoor demonstrations and meetings until December 10. All meetings, whether for or against the Constitution, had to be held indoors and required the previous permission of the provincial electoral commission. An extra 1,500 Civil Guard members were sent to the Basque country on November 30. In the rest of Spain, the armed forces were charged with maintaining security and order during the referendum.

On December 6, Spanish voters demonstrated that the framers of the Constitution succeeded in writing a document acceptable to the majority of the country. Of all eligible voters, 67.7 percent went to the polls, and 87.8 percent of those casting a ballot voted "yes"; only 7.9 percent voted "no," while 4.3 percent cast blank, or null, ballots. Thus 59.4 percent of all eligible voters voted "yes." The results were not so overwhelmingly favorable as in the December 1976 referendum, when 73.2 percent of eligible voters cast a "yes" ballot. The degree of approval was, however, impressive for three reasons: this was the third time Spaniards had been called to the polls in two years; it was widely believed that the Constitution would be easily approved and that, therefore, there was little need to vote; and a detailed text was bound to alienate more people than a general proposal for democratic reform like that presented two years earlier.

There were few surprises in the results. Outside Galicia and the Basque country, participation rates and the proportion of "yes" votes varied relatively little from province to province (see Table 6.1). The conservative parts of Castile, which had voted more heavily for the Popular Alliance in the June 1977 election, showed a higher percentage of "no" votes, but in every province outside the Basque country, "no" votes tallied less than 15 percent. Far-right opposition to democracy made a weak showing even in such strongholds as Palencia, Toledo, Guadalajara, and Burgos. The referendum confirmed once more that Francoism had died with the death of the Caudillo, if not earlier.

Extremely low participation rates in Galicia (Orense, 40.5 percent; Lugo, 43.6 percent; La Coruña, 54.5 percent) reflected not a protest against the new Constitution but the peculiar economic, social, and political conditions that have led a large proportion of the region's inhabitants to abstain in every election during the twentieth century. Relatively few

TABLE 6.1

Provincial Results of Referendum, December 1978

Province	Percent That Voted	Yes	No	Blank and Null
		(Percent of registered voters)		
National	67.7	87.8	7.9	4.3
Alava	59.2	71.4	19.2	9.4
Albacete	71.9	88.3	7.8	3.9
Alicante	72.4	89.7	6.7	3.5
Almería	67.1	92.8	4.8	2.5
Avila	74.5	89.0	6.6	4.5
Badajoz	72.5	88.9	7.8	3.3
Baleares	70.4	89.5	4.8	5.7
Barcelona	68.6	90.4	4.7	4.9
Burgos	72.2	81.5	12.6	5.9
Cáceres	69.3	89.7	6.8	3.5
Cádiz	69.9	92.0	4.8	3.1
Castellón	78.8	88.4	7.0	4.6
Ciudad Real	70.2	85.1	11.0	3.9
Córdoba	75.1	90.8	6.5	2.7
Cuenca	74.8	84.8	11.4	3.7
Gerona	72.6	89.8	4.4	5.8
Granada	69.3	91.6	5.9	2.5
Guadalajara	76.1	81.4	14.1	4.4
Guipúzcoa	43.4	63.9	19.8	16.3
Huelva	69.6	92.6	4.4	3.0
Huesca	74.5	90.4	4.8	4.8
Jaén	72.7	88.9	8.7	2.4
La Coruña	54.5	89.7	5.3	5.0
León	65.5	88.1	6.6	5.3
Lérida	66.9	91.3	3.9	4.8
Logroño	75.2	86.6	7.8	5.6
Lugo	43.6	88.8	5.7	5.6
Madrid	72.3	86.9	10.2	2.9
Málaga	67.6	90.7	6.3	3.0
Murcia	71.3	90.8	6.2	3.0
Navarre	66.6	75.7	20.0	4.4
Orense	40.5	90.0	6.1	4.0
Oviedo	61.5	88.6	8.4	2.9
Palencia	74.3	79.1	14.9	6.0
Las Palmas	71.9	90.9	4.7	4.4

Pontevedra	55.2	88.1	6.5	5.3
Salamanca	75.8	88.2	6.2	5.6
Santa Cruz de				
Tenerife	57.7	93.1	3.9	3.0
Santander	71.3	83.3	12.7	4.0
Segovia	77.1	85.9	7.4	6.7
Seville	72.3	92.7	4.8	2.5
Soria	73.5	87.6	6.8	5.6
Tarragona	70.0	91.0	4.4	4.6
Teruel	74.0	85.9	8.4	5.6
Toledo	78.5	81.8	14.4	3.8
Valencia	76.4	88.6	7.1	4.4
Valladolid	75.0	82.5	11.5	6.0
Vizcaya	43.9	70.9	21.6	7.5
Zamora	69.9	83.5	9.5	7.0
Zaragoza	73.0	88.0	6.8	5.2
Ceuta	67.5	88.2	8.4	3.4
Melilla	67.7	88.5	8.5	3.1

Source: Informaciones (Madrid), December 7, 1978, and Europa Press, December 7, 1978.

Galicians bothered to vote, but a higher percentage of those who did so cast "yes" ballots than in the rest of the nation.

The results in Catalonia demonstrate clearly the success of Suárez's policies in that region. During the months before the referendum, Catalans complained loudly and often about the slowness with which the *Generalitat* was moving toward significant autonomy; but Table 6.2 shows that voters in all four Catalan provinces are prepared to work within the framework of the new Constitution. Particularly striking is the small number of "no" votes in Catalonia. This low percentage reflects three realities: Catalan nationalists have accepted the Constitution; the far right is weak in Catalonia; and the far left can mobilize little more support there than in the rest of the country.

The picture in the Basque country is more complex; in fact, is not a single picture at all (see Table 6.3). As we have pointed out, the PNV urged its followers not to reject a democratic Constitution with a "no" vote, but, rather, to register a protest against limitations on Basque autonomy by abstaining or casting a blank ballot. In Table 6.4 we have a rough estimate of this "positive" abstention, calculated as the rate of abstentions and blank votes over and above the national average. The picture which emerges confirms what we already knew about the strength

TABLE 6.2

Catalonia: Referendum Results, December 1978

Province	Percent of Registered Voters That Voted	Yes	No	Blank and Null	Abstained	Yes	No	Blank and Null
		(Percent of votes cast)				(Percent of voters registered)		
Barcelona	68.6	90.4	4.7	4.9	31.4	62.0	3.3	3.3
Gerona	72.6	89.8	4.4	5.8	27.4	65.2	3.2	4.2
Lérida	66.9	91.3	3.9	4.8	33.1	61.1	2.6	3.2
Tarragona	70.0	91.0	4.4	4.6	30.0	63.7	3.1	3.2
Spanish national average	67.7	87.8	7.9	4.3	32.3	59.4	5.4	2.9

Source: Author's calculation from data provided by Europa Press, December 7, 1978.

TABLE 6.3

Basque Country: Referendum Results, December 1978

Province	Percent of Registered Voters That Voted	Yes	No	Blank and Null	Abstained	Yes	No	Blank and Null
		(Percent of votes cast)				(Percent of voters registered)		
Alava	59.2	71.4	19.1	9.4	40.8	42.3	11.3	5.6
Guipúzcoa	43.5	63.9	19.8	16.3	56.5	27.8	8.6	7.1
Navarre	66.6	75.7	20.0	4.8	33.4	50.4	13.3	2.9
Vizcaya	43.9	70.9	21.6	7.5	56.1	31.1	9.5	3.3
Spanish national average	67.7	87.8	7.9	4.3	32.3	59.4	5.4	2.9

Source: Author's calculation from data provided by Europa Press, December 7, 1978.

TABLE 6.4

Basque Country: "Positive" Abstention in December 1978 Referendum

Province	"Positive" Abstention* (Percent of registered voters)	PNV Vote, June 1977 (Percent of registered voters)
Alava	11.2	14.1
Guipúzcoa	28.4	24.9
Navarre	1.1	6.7
Vizcaya	24.2	24.0

*"Positive" abstention = (percent of Basque voters abstaining − national average percent abstaining) + (percent of Basque voters casting blank ballots − national average percent casting blank ballots).

Source: Author's calculation from electoral statistics, *Diario 16* (Madrid), July 22, 1977; and referendum results supplied by Europa Press, December 7, 1978.

of moderate Basque nationalism in Guipúzcoa and Vizcaya, its relative weakness in Alava, and extreme weakness in Navarre. We cannot calculate here the number of voters who stayed away from the polls for fear of ETA violence, but this certainly contributed to the high rate of abstention in Guipúzcoa and Vizcaya.

The uniform proportion of "no" votes in the four Basque provinces is a result of quite different political realities. "No" ballots were cast in varying proportions in the four provinces by right-wing extremists, *abertzale* Basque nationalists (especially strong in Guipúzcoa and Vizcaya), and other fringe groups of the extreme left. In Navarre some of the "no" votes must also have come from Navarrese nationalists who were disgruntled over the Constitutions's attempt to force them into becoming part of the Basque region. In view of the strength of the far left, the far right, and Navarrese nationalists in the province, it seems surprising that the "no" vote in Navarre was not considerably higher than 20 percent. Many far-left partisans who would otherwise have voted "no" must have cast "yes" ballots because of the Constitution's provisions for including Navarre in the Basque country.

In the Basque country it is particularly important to look closely not only at the percentage of votes cast for and against the Constitution, but at the percentage of eligible voters involved. "Yes" votes accounted for 63.8 percent of the ballots cast in Guipúzcoa, but only 27.8 percent of eligible voters in the province voted for the Constitution. A close look at these results suggests that winning over the Basques may prove even more difficult than it previously appeared.

GENERAL CHARACTERISTICS

In the nineteenth century, constitutions came and went in Spain with every change of the political balance. Each group that obtained power wrote a constitution to fit its own needs and ideals, only to see it modified or discarded by its successors in office. A desire to avoid a repetition of that pattern lay at the root of the concern for achieving a consensus which so strongly affected the entire character of this Constitution.

Consensus could, perhaps, have been achieved by limiting the Constitution to broad principles with which most could agree, avoiding all reference to specific issues over which controversy was sure to arise. The drafters, however, did not choose this route. Rather they dealt at length and in detail with controversial issues, but deliberately employed ambiguous language which could be interpreted to suit the desires of different groups. This technique certainly facilitated obtaining an overwhelming vote in favor of the text, but will cause serious problems of interpretation if the Constitution remains in effect for any length of time.

A desire to facilitate consensus by including in the Constitution something for everyone explains the document's length (169 articles and 15,000 words) as well as the presence of numerous statements of principle that have no direct practical effect on the country's future. The drafters hoped to win the support of young voters, for instance, by including an article which stated that "the authorities will promote conditions for the free and effective participation of youth in political, social, economic, and cultural development." Older citizens were promised that the state "will promote their well-being through a system of social services that will take care of their specific problems of health, housing, culture, and leisure." These were, however, merely pious wishes with no substantive content. They required no specific action from the government and established no rights. The Constitution itself explicitly states that none of these "governing principles of political, economic, and social life" that comprise Articles 35 to 47 can form the basis for litigation in the courts except "through the procedures in the laws that develop them." Unless, therefore, a future Cortes passes legislation that reflects these principles, they will have no practical effect on the country's life.

PARLIAMENTARY MONARCHY

The new constitution stipulates that "the political form of the Spanish state is a parliamentary monarchy." The king "is the head of state and symbol of its unity and permanence." He represents Spain in its dealings with foreign countries, sanctions and promulgates laws, and is commander-in-chief of the armed forces. In addition to these representative functions, he plays a potentially crucial political role in the designation of the President of the Government. Whenever a new President of the Government must be named, it is up to the king to nominate a candidate after consulting with the representatives of the political parties, unless the previous government fell on a motion of censure, in which case the name of the new President would be indicated in the motion of censure. If the first candidate cannot win a vote of confidence, the king will propose another until eventually someone does obtain the confidence of the deputies. If after two months no candidate has been able to win the confidence of the Congress of Deputies, the king will dissolve the Cortes and call new elections. This is the king's most important political power. He does not have the authority to extend the life of the legislature beyond its constitutional limits, nor can he dissolve it except at the proposal of the President of the Government.

Both the PSOE and the PCE are republican in ideology and tradition. Their leaders recognized, however, that voting to establish a republic would alarm the army and the conservatives, seriously divide the country, destroy the constitutional consensus, and prove futile, since the UCD and the AP hold enough votes to thwart any such attempt. Both González and Carillo made it clear from the beginning that they would accept a monarchy despite their preference for a republic. The PCE, which has consistently adopted a flexible, pragmatic line, was even willing to vote for the monarchy. The PSOE abstained from voting on the paragraph of Article 1 which declares that: "The political form of the Spanish state is a parliamentary monarchy, " but it carefully explained that it would loyally support a monarchy once it was established. This understanding was the foundation of the consensus among the parties that underlay the entire drafting of the Constitution.

The Constitution establishes a bicameral legislature called the Cortes. The lower chamber, called the Congress of Deputies, is to have between 300 and 400 members, elected by "free, equal, direct, and secret universal suffrage" for a period of four years. The provinces will be the electoral districts. At the insistence of the UCD, Article 68 provides that the electoral law must establish some minimum initial number of deputies for each district before distributing the rest in proportion to population. This provision guarantees overrepresentation of the rural areas where the UCD is strongest. The PSOE agreed to fixing a minimum number of deputies per province in return for the UCD's approval of a clause requiring proportional representation within each province. The Socialists' determination to establish proportional representation in the Constitution itself reflects their fears that a majority system would inexorably force them into a formal alliance with the PCE. A major political battle remains to be fought over the electoral law that will specify the exact number of deputies, the minimum number per province, and the details of the system of proportional representation. On the outcome of that battle will depend in large part the balance of forces in any future Cortes.

The shape of the future Senate underwent profound transformations in the course of the constitutional debates. In the first subcommittee draft, senators appeared as representatives of the regions and other autonomous communities, elected by their legislative assemblies. The Deputies gradually transformed the upper house into a body composed of four members from each province, chosen directly by the citizens, plus an almost purely nominal two representatives of each region. The Senators strengthened slightly the link between the upper chamber and the autonomous communities, but the final text of the constitution calls for a Senate composed primarily of members chosen by the voters of each province. The legislative assembly of each region will designate one Senator plus one for each one million inhabitants of the region. This means that only about 20 percent of the Senators will be chosen by the regional assemblies.

The legislative initiative lies with the government, the Congress of Deputies, and the Senate. The assemblies of the regions can submit projects to the government or to the Congress of Deputies, but cannot initiate legislation at the national level. The Constitution calls for legislation to be drafted to permit popular initiative with a minimum of 500,000 signatures.

Almost all legislative authority rests with the Congress of Deputies. Bills passed by it must be submitted to the Senate for approval, but the Congress can override the Senate's veto by a vote of a simple majority of its members. Only in cases of a closely divided Congress will the Senate, in which the conservative rural provinces will be heavily overrepresented, be able to oppose an effective veto. If a party or coalition holds a solid majority in the Congress of Deputies, it will be able virtually to ignore the Senate, except for whatever effects its veto might have on public opinion. The Senate must always give its opinion within two months and can be required to do so in twenty days, so it does not even have the power to delay legislation significantly.

The executive authority is vested in the government, made up of a president nominated by the king and of vice presidents, ministers, and other members named by the president. Members of the government need not necessarily be deputies. The government is collectively responsible to the Congress of Deputies, but at the UCD's insistence it is in a strong position vis-à-vis the deputies since a motion of censure must contain the name of a candidate who will automatically succeed the president if the motion is approved. This requirement of a constructive censure, taken from the West German Constitution, will make over-throwing a government much more difficult, especially since minority parties are likely to hold a significant number of seats for the foreseeable future. It may lead to situations of deadlock in which the government does not have a majority but cannot be overthrown since the opposition cannot agree beforehand on the name of a new president.

The judicial power is vested in independent courts. The Constitution prohibits extraordinary political tribunals and limits the jurisdiction of military courts to members of the armed services except during a state of siege. It makes no provision for the naming of judges, which will be regulated by a later law. Constitutional questions will be resolved not by the Supreme Court, but by a special Constitutional Court, made up of 12 judges, named for a nine-year period. Four are to be nominated by a three-fifths vote of the Congress, four by a three-fifths vote of the Senate, two by the government, and two by the General Council of the Judiciary. The vagueness and ambiguity of many constitutional provisions guarantee the Constitutional Court a key role in the future development of Spanish life. Since one-third of its members will be nominated by a Senate which presumably will be considerably more conservative than the Congress of Deputies, the Constitutional Court may well prove to be an important power position for Spanish conservatives, especially if the Suárez government appoints judges prior to holding new political elections.

REGIONAL AUTONOMY

Much discussion was required to arrive at the exact wording of the abstract statement about the relations between center and periphery at the beginning of the Constitution. The most extreme Basque regionalists demanded that the Constitution recognize the right of "self-determination" of Spain's constituent national groups, but that proposal obtained little support. Even the Basque Nationalist Party refused to vote for it. At the other extreme, conservatives objected to any mention of regional autonomy, but they too were a tiny minority. There was a general consensus that the Constitution would have to grant regional autonomy and that it would also defend the indivisibility of the country.

In final form, Article 2 states that: "The Constitution is based on the indissoluble unity of the Spanish nation, the common and indivisible fatherland of all Spaniards, and recognizes and guarantees the right to autonomy of the nationalities and regions that make it up as well as the solidarity amongst them all." This wording was a compromise between centralists who objected to the use of the word "nationalities" to describe the outlying regions and regionalists who disliked the article's stress on the indivisibility of Spain.

The following article establishes "Castilian or Spanish" as the "official language of the state," and affirms the right of all Spaniards to use it and their duty to know it. It stipulates, however, that the other languages of Spain will also be official in the corresponding regions, and promises that linguistic diversity will be respected and protected as part of the country's cultural patrimony.

The Constitution severely limits the jurisdiction of the future regions. Article 149 enumerates 32 areas which belong to the exclusive jurisdiction of the state. Among the most important are: basic conditions that guarantee the equality of all Spaniards and the exercise of their rights; international affairs; defense; justice; commercial, penal, labor, and civil law; foreign trade and tariffs; control of the monetary and banking system; general economic planning; social security; public safety; and general norm on education. Regions may in their statutes take jurisdiction over any areas not specifically reserved to the state. If this were to be the full extent of their authority, it would be limited indeed, but the Constitution provides, in addition, that the state may delegate by law part of its authority in areas reserved to its jurisdiction. The framers of the Constitution have, then, designed a system which gives the regions extremely limited primary authority, but allows it to be expanded by subsequent delegation.

The Constitution is only slightly less limiting about the financial resources of the regions. They may collect surtaxes or taxes ceded to them by the state as well as impose taxes of their own and take out loans. The state, however, reserves the right to regulate their activity. To help mitigate the differences between rich and poor regions, the Constitution foresees the establishment of an interterritorial compensation investment fund to be financed out of general revenues. The disparity in wealth of the various future regions will make it necessary for the state to take other measures to control their financial activities if Spain is to move toward any sort of equitable economic balance.

The mechanisms foreseen for establishing regions are extremely complex, and were the subjects of heated debate. In essense they will permit Catalonia, the Basque country, Galicia, and a few other areas to develop quickly, while guaranteeing that during the first five years the government of regions in which there is little enthusiasm for autonomy will have very limited authority.

As a concession to Basque nationalists, the Committee on Constitutional Affairs of the Congress of Deputies added an additional clause which declared that: "The Constitution protects and respects the historic rights of the territories which enjoyed *fueros* [special statutes and liberties dating from the Middle Ages]. Those special rights will be exercised, when applicable, in the framework of the Constitution and of their autonomy statutes." This clause had little specific content and was added merely to please the Basques, but they angrily rejected it. The *fueros*, they argued, were part of their patrimony, and depended for their legitimacy not on the Constitution and the autonomy statutes, but on historic precedent. As noted above, the Senate Committee on Constitutional Affairs briefly reopened the question by approving a Basque-sponsored amendment that eliminated the specific reference to the constitutional framework. The full Senate rejected the amendment, and in any case, the additional clause was included in the Constitution in its original form over Basque opposition.

INDIVIDUAL RIGHTS AND PUBLIC LIBERTIES

The Constitution opens with 52 articles that establish the general outlines of the new Spanish state and define the rights of its citizens and the principles that will inspire its activities. Citizens are guaranteed the full range of liberal personal rights and equality before the law regardless of "birth, race, sex, religion, opinion, or any other personal or social circumstance." The Constitution prohibits the death penalty except in military trials in time of war, establishes freedom of the press without any form of prior censorship, admits conscientious objection to military service, and recognizes the right to work. At many points, the principles enunciated are the exact antithesis of the Franco regime: autonomy for the outlying regions; political parties as an expression of democratic pluralism; and trade unions, for example.

The violent, bitter anti-clericalism that divided Spaniards so sharply during the debates on the Constitution of the Second Republic in 1931 has dissipated, but the position of the Church in society and its influence on education and family policy aroused heated controversy during the drafting and revision of this Constitution. The Socialists, the Communists, and other parties worked to outline a purely secular society in which the Church's influence on public life would be reduced to a minimum. The UCD and other Catholic forces struggled to retain a special place for the Church.

Article 15 guarantees religious freedom and the right to profess and manifest any creed or ideology, with no limitations other than those required by public order protected by the law. These provisions won the virtually unanimous approval of both laicists and Catholics alike. The article goes on to deny the character of state religion to any confession, but stipulates that the authorities "will take into account the religious beliefs of Spanish society and will, therefore, maintain relations with the Catholic Church and other confessions." The Church lobbied hard for this clause, and the UCD obtained this explicit mention of the Catholic Church only over bitter opposition. The Communist Party voted for the clause which, it said, created no new obligations for the state and simply recognized the *de facto* influence of the Church in Spanish life. The Socialists, however, refused to accept it, and abstained during the vote on the paragraph.

Another battle was waged over Article 27, which deals with education. The points at issue involved religion, but the debate reflected broader divergencies about the aims of education and the structure of society. The UCD and its allies defended a diversified educational system in which groups of parents and other private citizens would play a leading role. The state would not only permit private schools but would aid and assist them as a contribution to the pluralism which the opening articles of the Constitution listed among the values that inspire the new Spanish state. Citing the United Nations 1948 Declaration of Human Rights, proponents of this view argued that parents have a primary responsibility in education and have a corresponding right to determine the type of education they want for their children. The function of the state, they continued, is to aid and assist parents in fulfilling their responsibility, to provide whatever levels of public education are necessary to insure that all citizens can in fact exercise their right to education, and to guarantee certain basic minimum standards in all schools, whether public or private.

The Socialists, to the contrary, viewed the state as having primary responsibility in education. They did not deny the right of parents or other groups of citizens to found private schools, but they disliked the idea of their receiving government aid and favored a high degree of government control over the curriculum and day-to-day functioning of all schools. They admitted the right of parents to choose the type of education their children would receive, but argued that this right could best be exercised through the influence of parents' associations on public schools. This position implied a reversal with respect to the Socialists' position on political representation. In the political field, the Socialists consistently attacked majority rule as providing insufficient protection to minorities, but in education they showed little concern for the rights or desires of those dissatisfied with the decisions of the state and of the majority of parents.

The positions of both sides were, of course, strongly influenced not only by the abstract principles they enunciated but also by the social realities of Spanish education. The vast majority of private schools in Spain are Church-related, and affluent Spaniards have traditionally sent their children to private primary and secondary schools. (The state has long had a virtual monopoly on university education. The University of Navarre is the only full-fledged private university in the country.) In the eyes of the Socialists, then, private education implied both religious influence on public life and a way for the upper and middle classes to obtain a superior education for their children.

The final text of Article 27 is the result of heated debates and painful compromises. Like most of the provisions on controversial questions it is extremely ambiguous and leaves the door open to divergent and even contradictory policies. The UCD obtained the support of the Socialists for a paragraph guaranteeing the rights of parents to see to it that their children "receive religious and moral training in accord with their own convictions." In addition it succeeded in including in an earlier article the stipulation that "norms relating to fundamental rights and liberties recognized by the Constitution will be interpreted it conformity with the Universal Declaration of Human Rights." This will permit it to defend the primacy of parents' rights in education as recognized by the 1948 UN declaration. It also won approval of a paragraph that recognized the right "of physical and moral persons to found centers of instruction," but failed in its attempt to extend this right to "directing" as well as "founding" schools.

Many Socialists favored giving teachers and students a major voice in the running of schools. The question is particularly critical in the schools founded and run by religious orders and other private centers where groups of teachers have been attempting to increase their influence. The Constitution provides that "teachers, parents, and where appropriate, students, will take part in the control and operation of the centers supported by the government with public funds, in the terms established by law." There will undoubtedly be much controversy in the future both over the legislation which will specify how this right is to be exercised and over what amount of financial aid to a private school constitutes "support."

Another paragraph stipulates that the government *will* (not merely *may* as the Socialists wished) provide financial assistance to schools which meet the requirements set by law, but in the absence of any provision about the level of aid, UCD's victory here may prove purely illusory.

While the Church in the area of education had to settle for ambiguous compromises whose ultimate outcome will depend on the future composition both of the Cortes and of the Constitutional Court, in the area of family law, it suffered a number of clear defeats. The Constitution avoids use the word "divorce," but provides that the law will regulate the "causes of separation and dissolution." Efforts to obtain a right-to-life clause or some other form of constitutional prohibition of abortion also failed.

In addition to defining individual liberties, the Constitution also lays down "principles governing economic and social policy." Once again the fundamental differences that divided the PSOE from the UCD led to a series of compromises. The Constitution stipulates a system of private property and inheritance, conditioned by their "social function." It provides for a market economy, but also for "public initiative in the economy." The government is charged with the obligation of pursuing a policy that insures economic stability and full employment. It is given the right to reserve to the public sector vital resources and services and to control certain businesses in the public interest, but is not required by the Constitution to exercise those rights. Similarly, economic planning is authorized but not called for. The Socialists failed to obtain some of the provisions which they had initially hoped for, such as a clause calling for a statute regulating worker participation in business decision-making. Similarly, business interests failed to obtain a clause which would have granted them the right to dismiss workers who were no longer needed. The Constitution does not, however, contain provisions that would prohibit legislation in these fields. Its text seems flexible enough to allow both Socialist and non-Socialist governments to implement their economic programs without requiring them to undertake any activities to which they might object.

CONSTITUTIONAL REFORM

Initiative in constitutional reform belongs to the government, the Congress of Deputies, and the Senate. The regions, and the people via a petition can request a constitutional amendment, but cannot initiate it. Amendments require a three-fifths majority of both houses and will be submitted to referendum if one-tenth of the deputies or senators so request. If a proposed amendment is approved by a majority of the Senate but fails to win the support of three-fifths of the senators it may be passed by a two-thirds vote of the Congress of Deputies.

A special, more stringent, procedure has been established for proposals of total reform of the Constitution and for amendments which modify its provisions about the basic characteristics of the state (Articles 1–9), public liberties (Articles 15–29), and the Crown (Articles 56–65). If such proposals receive the approval of two-thirds of both chambers, the Cortes will immediately be dissolved and new elections held. If the new Cortes again approves the measures by a two-thirds majority they will be submitted to a national referendum.

In the area of ordinary legislation, the Senate has been given almost no power, but it could be a significant factor in the field of constitutional reform. It will be a distinctly more conservative body than the Congress of Deputies. At least in the immediate future, conservatives should be able to find two-fifths of the Senators to oppose attempts to transform the Constitution in a more socialistic direction. It is unlikely that the Socialists would be able to muster in the foreseeable future the two-thirds majority of the Congress of Deputies that would be necessary to override such opposition.

As it now stands, the Constitution seems flexible enough to allow any foreseeable Spanish government to carry out its programs with little hindrance, but much will depend on the decisions of the Constitutional Court. If that body interprets the Constitution in a broad, nonrestrictive sense, there should be little need for constitutional amendment. If, however, the Court reads it in a narrow sense, a future Socialist government might find itself seriously embarrassed by constitutional prohibitions. In that case the highly restrictive mechanisms established for amending the Constitution would prove counterproductive. Rather than contributing to constitutional stability, they would constitute an inducement to reject the entire document.

7

CONCLUSIONS

The speed and relative ease with which the transformations we have discussed in this book took place are puzzling in view of the strength and stability of the Franco regime even during the final years of the dictator's life. Down to his final days, he stood in no real danger of being overthrown, yet only three years later the institutions he created had all but disappeared. This contrast can be understood only in terms of the nature of the support which contributed to the regime's stability and of the process by which it was transformed.

During the last decade or more of its existence, the regime benefited from the widespread expectation that Franco would not live much longer. Many opponents felt that it was futile to try to overthrow him when in a few years at most he was certain to die. Although Franco did not hesitate to treat his opponents harshly, the stability of his regime in its final years rested not only on the strength of the police and the army, but also on a kind of passive acceptance based on the expectation of the dictator's proximate demise.

The Franco regime, as we have seen, had very little ideological content at any point in its long course. People supported the regime not because they believed in the principles of the Falange or later of the National Movement, but for more pragmatic motives. The regime's initial legitimacy came from its victory in the Civil War. Subsequently this was supplemented and to a degree displaced by success in economic development and in maintaining peace. At Franco's death, there were few significant forces committed to the maintenance of the political structure of his regime. The employees of the syndicates and others members of the state bureaucracy had, of course, a vested interest in their jobs, but little or no loyalty to the institutions they had served.

Material for this chapter was taken from "A Threat to Spanish Democracy," by John F. Coverdale, New York *Times*, August 3, 1978. Copyright 1978 by The New York Times Company. Reprinted by permission.

Like the dictatorship of Primo de Rivera, the Franco regime had gradually lost support even among its own natural clients. Thirty years after the fall of the Fascist regimes that had inspired its rhetoric and its choreography, many Spaniards felt vaguely embarrassed by the political apparatus of their country. The National Movement, the vertical syndicates, and the authoritarian structure of the Franco system seemed out of keeping with the times and unsuited to a country which had undergone rapid industrialization and urbanization.

Memories of the horrors of the Civil War helped to stabilize Franco's regime by dissuading his opponents from trying to overthrow him. Strangely enough, after his death they became a potent force for a spirit of reconciliation, moderation, and compromise. Political leaders of almost all persuasions have shown a determination to avoid the polarization that led to the bloody Civil War in the 1930s. The parties of the left learned then the dangers of underestimating the strength of conservatism and of pursuing maximalist policies which could provoke right-wing reaction. Younger conservatives, for their part, have proven anxious to search for common grounds, to find ways of legitimizing their government so that it rests not on armed strength but on genuine popular consensus. Almost all political groups except those of the extreme Fascist right have tacitly agreed not to talk about the war and its atrocities, and not to mention the collaboration of many politicians with the regime born of Franco's victory in that war. Both the Church and the army for their parts have been anxious to avoid the direct involvement in politics which helped to precipitate the Civil War.

From outside the country came considerable pressure for democratization. Western European countries whose approval Spain sought all had more liberal and democratic regimes. In various ways, they attempted to move Spain to adopt political forms more in keeping with their own. Specifically, they made democratization a condition for Spanish entrance into the Common Market. Subsequent events have clearly revealed that other countries frequently used the excuse of Spain's authoritarian regime so as not to have to mention their economic objections to her joining the Common Market. At the time of Franco's death, however, most Spaniards and particularly Spanish businessmen believed that democratization would open the doors of the EEC to them.

Many opposition groups in Spain were less committed to the political freedom of a liberal democratic regime than to the social and economic equality that is the goal of European socialism. The experience of Franco's long-lived authoritarian regime, however, made these groups at least temporarily sensitive to the practical advantages of what their ideologues would have described as "merely bourgeois liberties." Virtually the entire opposition understood that Spain had to construct a democratic political system before any serious thought could be given to social and economic transformation of the country. Spain did not face any grave, pressing external crisis like that which Portugal experienced in Africa. The sheer duration of Franco's repression, however, had been sufficient to mold a broad national consensus on the necessity for democratic institutions despite serious divergences about the desired future shape of the political and economic structure.

We have stressed repeatedly the significance of the generational change in Spain's political leadership for understanding its transformation. The Franco regime had lasted so long that there was no question of *restoring* the institutions of the Republic. Except for a few isolated figures, the leaders of the Republic were all dead. Only the Communist Party and one faction of the Christian Democrats had among their leaders outstanding figures from the pre-Franco period. The change went deeper, however. The new leadership not only did not hark back to the Republic. It skipped over an entire generation of men between 50 and 65. The new leaders of Spain were mostly men in their forties, contemporaries of King Juan Carlos.

This sudden renewal of political leadership created a sharp disjunction between political and economic power. The heads of the large financial and industrial concerns, like the commanders of the army, are generally 15 to 20 years older than the political leaders. Why didn't these older men who had benefited greatly during the Franco era and who still wielded great economic power, try to use it to prevent political change? The answer lies in their experience during the last two decades.

During the Franco era, business leaders, like top military commanders, were profoundly depoliticized. They benefited from many of the regime's policies, but took little interest in political life. They were content to leave politics to the politicians and to attend to their business. These attitudes carried over into the post-Franco era. Business leaders protested vigorously against certain proposals which seemed to threaten their control of their businesses, but otherwise they took little interest in politics.

In addition, as we have seen, the new Spanish managerial class, created by the economic prosperity of the 1960s, was convinced that democratic institutions were necessary for the future stability of the country. They were opposed to any form of socialism, but recognized that the authoritarian methods of the Franco regime were unsuited to Spain's new situation and to the Western European environment in which they would like to see the country move.

We have stressed the importance of the gradual nature of political change, especially in disarming potential opposition from the army and other extreme right elements. To some extent, President Suárez and King Juan Carlos may themselves have been deceived by their own gradualism. They seem to have underestimated at first the strength and resiliency of the leftist opposition and to have thought that it could be placated with measures less sweeping than those they were eventually forced to undertake. It may well be that had they foreseen the full extent of the changes they would have to institute, they might have resisted more firmly at an earlier stage. They themselves, however, did not know what the future would hold, and have been moved forward gradually by pressure from the left.

Political analysts viewing the situation immediately prior to Franco's death asked how any prospective liberalizing politician could circumvent such strongholds of Francoism as the Council of the Realm and the Cortes. One of the most surprising features of this political transformation is that its authors have not circumvented but rather utilized those institutions for their own ends. Suárez demonstrated extraordinary political ability in convincing the central institutions of the Franco regime not only to accept but to give their stamp of approval to changes which in fact signified their own demise. This was made possible in large part by the lack of ideological commitment that characterized the final years and even decades of the regime's existence. It was also facilitated by the efforts of King Juan Carlos who, as Franco's designated successor, exercised considerable authority over those who did feel any personal loyalty to Franco or to his regime.

The collaboration of the Council of the Realm and of the last Franco Cortes was vital for giving the new institutions legitimacy in the eyes of the army and other conservative forces. Had the changes been carried out by decree or referendum without the approval of the Cortes, they almost undoubtedly would have met much stiffer opposition from conservatives within the army. The collaboration of the Cortes deprived a possible right-wing opposition of a great deal of its political legitimacy.

Five men have played vital roles in this process of political transformation: King Juan Carlos, President Suárez, General Guttíerez Mellado, Torcuato Fernández Miranda, and Santiago Carillo. The king's role has been highlighted throughout this book. He has been to a very large degree the moving force behind political change. Although trained and selected by Franco, Juan Carlos early recognized that liberalization of Spain's political structures was essential to his continuing on the throne as well as to the tranquility of the country. He demonstrated ability in finding men who were ready and able to carry out his wishes without provoking the right to a violent reaction. In addition, his close personal ties with the armed forces have been extremely important in maintaining their loyalty in the face of political change and terrorist attacks against their members.

President Suárez fits into the historical category of conservative modernizers whose most outstanding representative is Otto von Bismarck. Like Bismarck, Suárez is a man of few ideological commitments.

He believes in a hierarchical society and in the principles of private property, but has little or no interest in preserving the past for its own sake. Also like Bismarck, Suárez is committed principally to maintaining his own power and that of the king he serves. Short of sacrificing the basic principles of a hierarchical society and of an economy founded on private property, he is willing to make whatever compromises may be necessary to ensure his own continuance in power. Finally, like the great German chancellor, he has demonstrated both a keen awareness of the political realities of the moment and a willingness and ability to form coalitions with whomever is willing to support him. Suárez has brought Spain further along the road to democracy than anyone expected of him at his nomination, and quite possibly further than he himself ever expected to go.

Fernández Miranda is by temperament and conviction a much more authentic conservative than Suárez, dedicated to the principles of an orderly hierarchical society. In sharp contrast to the president, he seems to have little or no personal political ambition. He was moved by loyalty to the king rather than by desire for personal success or by ideological commitment. It was precisely his combination of impeccable conservative credentials together with loyalty to the Crown which made it possible for him to guide through the Cortes critical measures which a man of more liberal talent might have been unable to convince that Francoist body to accept.

General Guttíerez Mellado performed for the Crown much the same services with respect to the army as Fernández Miranda had performed with respect to the Council of the Realm and the Cortes. On repeated occasions, he convinced his fellow officers to accept measures which many of the most influential generals found repugnant. In addition, he wielded his authority to discipline and replace dissident members of the military hierarchy before they could block reform measures.

Finally, mention must be made of the Communist leader Santiago Carillo. Under his leadership, the Spanish Communist Party has followed a moderate, flexible, pragmatic line which has greatly facilitated the government's reformist plans. Suárez could not have overcome army and other conservative opposition to legalization of a Communist Party which had seemed militant and revolutionary or which had merely refused to accept the monarchy. Without a legally recognized Communist Party, democratization from above would have seemed much more suspect in the eyes of the entire left and the center-left which might well have refused to cooperate as it had refused to accept legal status under Arias's legislation on political parties. The consensus which is essential to Suárez's approach to democratization could not, therefore, have been achieved without Carillo's moderate leadership of the PCE. Carillo was also instrumental in convincing the Workers' Commissions to accept the austerity package included in the Moncloa Pact. Without their collaboration, this economic policy would certainly have failed, and its failure might well have brought with it the end of efforts to institute democratic institutions.

Suárez devised and implemented a two-tiered strategy of political coalition. At the level of government, he formed a center-right coalition which provided a broad enough plurality to permit him to form a cabinet without including elements which would force him to make distasteful concessions. For elaboration of the Constitution, however, as well as in the field of economic policy, he in effect formed a much broader coalition, which amounted to a government of national unity. This strategy enabled him to retain the initiative which comes from controlling the government, while obtaining sufficiently broad support to offer some hope that the Constitution may prove a lasting document acceptable to most political forces.

With the help of an artificial "consensus" motivated by a widely-shared desire to achieve a "European" style government, Spain has succeeded in forging an acceptable set of democratic institutions. Now that the atmosphere of "consensus" is dissolving, Spaniards are confronted with the even more difficult task of making their new institutions work.

They now face a set of serious trials. One of the most difficult tests and among the most critical will be the ability of the government to find some acceptable solution to the country's economic problems. Inflation and balance of payments have been brought under control, but unemployment presents a serious and growing challenge whose political implications are vastly increased by the high percentage of young people among the unemployed. Thus far, Spaniards have proven extremely understanding of the difficulties facing their government, and they are willing to accept economic hardship in order to guarantee political freedom. They cannot be expected long to continue such forbearance. If the government does not succeed in reducing unemployment and stimulating further economic growth, disenchantment with democratic institutions is bound to grow.

Equally as pressing and as difficult as the economic challenge is the regional one, especially in the Basque country. Spain's leaders will need to show generosity and courage in dealing with the Basque provinces in order to win the support of large sectors of the population which are now neutral at best with regard to the government's struggle against extremist terrorism. If violence in the north is not to destabilize Spanish democracy, the government must move quickly to grant substantial autonomy to the Basques. Until a Basque police force can be created, the government must discipline and control the police. Moderate Basque leaders, for their part, must condemn extremism, and the autonomy they can achieve under the Constitution. They must also convince their constituents that if Navarre is brought in under duress, it will only threaten the future peace of the

Basque region. Unless the government moves quickly and Basque politicians strongly support moderate autonomy within the framework of the Constitution, the violence in the Basque country will continuue to threaten the future of Spanish democracy.

INDEX

ABC, 70

Abertzales, 67, 68, 75

abortion, 132

Abril Matorell, Fernando, 104, 115

Acció Catalana, 27

affective identification, 24, 30

agrarian reform, 92

Ajuriaguerra, Juan, 98

Alfonso XIII, King, 36

Algeria, 100

Alonso Vega, Camilo, 38

Alvarez de Miranda, Fernando, 62, 72, 82, 89

Amador Franco, Admiral Enrique, 58

Amendment of Constitution, 133–134

amnesty: at accession of Juan Carlos, 37, 38–39; demanded by common criminals, 83; demanded by opposition, 55; demonstrations for, 39, 48, 59, 87; as issue in electoral campaigns, 68; of July, 1976, 48; of March, 1977, 59; of October, 1977, 91; reasons for its importance, 13

Apalategui, Miguel Angel, 86

Apertura, 17

Aperturistas, 18

Arana y Goiri, Sabino de, 33

Areilza, José María de: and crisis of Arias's government, 44, 45; named Minister of Foreign Affairs, 38; political background of, 18, 44; and Popular Party, 62

Arévalo, Manuel Clavero. (*See*, Clavero Arévalo, Manuel)

Arias Navarro, Carlos: appraisal of government of, 43; attitude toward opposition, 40; background of, 37–38; confirmed as president of government by Juan Carlos, 37; deterioration of economy under, 42–43; forms government, 15, 38; and legislation on political associations, 17; policy statement by, 39; political reform during second government of, 40–42; promises greater openness, 17; reasons for fall of, 43–44; in senate election, 74; television press conference, 9–10

armed forces. (*See*, army)

armed police, 7–8, 60, 93, 106, 107

army: appointment of Fernández Miranda designed to tranquilize, 37; attitude of toward Suárez's reforms, 50–51; attitudes of officers of, 4, 6–7; code of military justice, 93–94; Juan Carlos makes overtures to, 36–37; leftist groups in, 7; opposition of to legalization of extreme-left parties, 58–59; political influence of, 7; and politics during Franco era, 4–8; reaction of to resignation of General de Santiago, 50; unrest in, 109. (*See also*, armed police and civil guard)

Arzallus, Xavier, 115

assembly: right of, 41, 94

Assembly of Basque Representatives, 86, 90, 97–98

Assembly of Catalan Representatives, 84, 85, 90

Assembly of Catalonia, 48

associations. (*See*, political associations)

Atares Peña, General Juan, 109 `

austerity: in Moncloa Pacts, 92–93

autonomy: of areas other than Catalonia and the Basque Country, 99–100; of Basque Country, 97–98; of Canary Islands, 99–100; constitutional provisions on, 116, 117, 128–130; demonstrations for, 39; history of in Spain, 25–26, 32; as issue in elections, 67, 68, 69; Statute of 1932, 84, 90. (*See also*, regionalism)

Babcock Wilcox, 99, 103
balance of payments, 46, 47, 87, 102–103, 110
Balearic Islands, 99
Bank of Navarre, 103
bank secrecy, 88
Barcelona, 1, 22, 27
Basque Council, 98, 107, 109
Basque Country: church support of regionalism in, 8; constitutional referendum in, 119, 121, 124; demands for recognition of sovereignty of, 99; demonstrations in, 39, 48, 59, 86, 87, 99; economy of, 29–30, 34–35, 99; electoral campaign in, 67–68; general characteristics of, 29–32; historical background of, 32–33; hostility toward civil guard in, 61–62; identification with, 30; immigration into, 30; industrialization in, 32; negotiations on autonomy for, 85, 90–91, 97–98; pacification of, 98, 108; pre-autonomy statute of, 98; population of, 28–29; results of elections in, 74–75; Spanish and French, 29; under Franco, 33; violence in, 61–62, 83
Basque language, 31–32, 33. (*See also*, regional languages)
Basque nationalism, 32–34
Basque Nationalist Action Party (ANV), 67
Basque Nationalist Party (PNV): its attitudes toward ETA, 107–108;

and election of president of Basque Council, 98; its electoral campaign, 67, 68; electoral results of, 75, 77; founding of, 33; and Lemóniz, 99; organizes march against violence, 107–108; proposes plan of pacification, 108; rejects demand for independence, 67; urges abstention in constitutional referendum, 118–119
Basque representatives, assembly of. (*See*, Assembly of Basque Representatives)
Basque Socialist Party (ESB), 67
Berlinguer, Enrico, 58
Bismarck, Otto von, 138
Brandt, Willy, 64
Burgo, Jaime Ignacio del, 97
business, 12–13, 102–103, 104, 137

Cabanillas, Pío, 9, 62, 63, 72
Caetano, Marcello, 43
Calvo Serer, Rafael, 9, 20
Calvo Sotelo, Leopoldo, 63, 82
Camacho, Marcelino, 89
Cambio 16, 70
Cambó, Francisco de Asís, 35
Camuñas, Ignacio, 62, 89
Canary Islands, 21, 99, 100–101
Cano, General Carlos Iniesta. (*See*, Iniesta Cano, General Carlos)
capital formation, 111
Carlism, 14, 32, 33, 118
Carrero Blanco, Admiral Luis, 4, 7, 15, 38, 106
Carrillo, Santiago, 19–20, 49, 57, 65, 104, 115, 139
Castellano, Pablo, 64
Catalan language, 22, 24, 25, 26, 27, 28, 34. (*See also*, regional languages)
Catalan Left (EC), 69
Catalan representatives, assembly of. (*See*, Assembly of Catalan Representatives)
Catalan Socialist Party, 69
Catalonia: Communists in, 74; consti-

tutional referendum in, 119, 121, 124; economy of, 22, 26, 27, 34–35; electoral campaign in, 68–69; electoral results in, 75, 77; *Generalitat* of, 27–28, 85–86, 90; history of, 21–25, 26, 27–28; immigration into, 22; population of, 22; regional sentiment in, 8, 22, 24–28; Tarradellas returns to, 84

censure: constitutional provisions on, 127–128

Center Democratic Union (UCD): on Basque issues, 67, 98; in Catalonia, 69; and Christian Democrats, 66; and constitutional provisions on education, 131–132; electoral campaign of, 63, 70, 71, 74; electoral results of, 71–73, 74, 77; formation of, 63, 70; pacts with PSOE on Constitution, 115; position of on electoral law, 126–127; rejects coalition government, 79; strains on, 89

centralism, 26–27, 27–28, 32, 35

Charles I, King, 25

Christian Democracy (DC), 45, 51, 54, 59, 62, 66, 69, 72, 77

Church: attitude of toward Constitution, 118–119; and Christian Democracy, 66; and Communist Party, 19; constitutional provisions on, 114, 130–132; and regional movements, 8; relations of with Franco, 8; and Workers' Commission, 11

civil guard, 7, 33, 60, 62, 93

civil war, 16, 28, 33, 135–136

Clavero Arévalo, Manuel, 83

Common Market. (*See*, European Economic Communities)

Communist Party (PCE): in Catalonia, 69; and Christians, 19; electoral campaign of, 64–65, 70; electoral results of, 74; during Franco regime, 11, 18–19; legalization of, 41, 48–50, 56–58, 65; modera-

tion of, 65; accepts Monarchy, 126; and Moncloa Pact, 93; renounces dictatorship of proletariat, 57; tactics of prior to legalization, 12, 18–20, 40, 51, 54–55, 56–57, 58–59; and Workers' Commissions, 65. (*See also*, Unified Socialist Party of Catalonia)

Communist Party of Euzkadi, 67

Communist Revolutionary League (LCR), 118

Confederation of Spanish Business Organizations, 104

Congress of Deputies: constitutional provisions on, 126–127

conscientious objection, 130

consensus: in preparation of Constitution, 113, 114–114, 116–117

Constituent Assembly, 40, 47, 50

Constitution: on censure, 127–128; on Church, 130–132; consensus on, 113–114, 115–117; Cortes votes on, 118; debate on in Congress of Deputies, 115–116; debate on in Senate, 116–118; drafts of, 113–115; on economic policy, 132–133; on education, 131–132; on form of government, 125–128; on judicial system, 128; provisions for amendment of, 133–134; quarrels between UCD and PSOE over, 114; referendum on, 118–125; on regional autonomy, 128–130; on regional languages, 129; on rights, 130–132

Constitutional Court, 128

Coordinación democrática. (*See*, Democratic Coordination)

corporativism, 11, 14

Cortes: Arias's proposals for reform of, 42; army's influence on, 7; debate censure of Minister of Interior, 89; constitutional provisions on, 126–127; control of expenditures by, 92; control of television by, 93; Fernández Miranda

named President of, 37–38; and
Franco, 138; and political parties,
41, 48, 79–80, 81; Suárez's pro-
posals for reform of, 50–51
Council of the Realm, 7, 37, 42, 138
coup: plan for thwarted, 109
courts: constitutional provisions on,
128
Cuadernos para el diálogo, 66, 70
Cuba, 27
Cubillo, Antonio, 100
Cunhal, Alvaro, 19
Czechoslovakia, 19

death penalty, 130
Democratic Assembly of the Basque
Country, 48
Democratic Center (CD), 62–63
democratic coordination, 39, 48, 49
Democratic Pact for Catalonia, 69, 77
demonstrations: for amnesty, 39, 48,
59, 86; attitude of government
toward, 40, 41; in Basque Country, 86, 97–98, 99; against violence, 60–61, 108–109; in
Vitoria, 39. (*See also*, public
order)
depoliticization, 12, 13
devaluation, 42–43, 87
Diada, 85
Díaz Alegría, Lt. General Manuel, 7
divorce, 132

economic conditions and policy, 1–4,
26, 27, 34–35, 42–43, 46–47, 82,
87–88, 92–93, 102–103, 110–
111, 132–133
education, 92, 114, 116–117, 131–132
elections, June 1977, 71–80
electoral law, 55–56, 95, 126–127
elites, 16, 33, 34
ETA V, 67, 84, 86, 91, 99, 106, 107–
108, 110
ethnicity, 34
Eurocommunism, 65
Europe, 17, 136–137
European Economic Communities,
12–13, 136
Euskera. (*See*, Basque language)
Euzkadi. (*See*, Basque Country)
exports, 102, 103

Falange Española, 14–15, 118, 135.
(*See also*, National Movement)
Fargas, Ramón Trias. (*See*, Trias
Fargas, Ramón)
Fascism, 14
February 12, Spirit of, 17
federalism, 67
Federation of Democratic and Liberal
Parties, 62
Federation of Socialist Parties, 64
Ferdinand, King of Aragon, 25
Fernández Miranda, Torcuato, 37,
43, 44, 51, 139
Fernández de la Mora, Gonzalo, 17,
118
Fernández Ordóñez, Francisco, 62,
72, 82, 104
Fernández-Urrutia, José Lladó y,
(*See*, Lladó y Fernández-Urrutia,
José)
First Carlist War, 32
fiscal policy reform, 43, 46–47, 87–88,
92
Foote, Michael, 64
Fraga Irribarne, Manuel, 9, 18, 38,
44, 45, 66, 115, 118
Franco, Admiral Enrique Amador.
(*See*, Amador Franco, Admiral
Enrique)
Franco y Bahamonde, Francisco, 1–
20 (*passim*), 63, 135–136
freedom march, Basque, 87
freedom of the press, 130
Freire, Lt. General Antonio Ibáñez.
(*See*, Ibáñez Freire, Lt. General
Antonio)
French Revolution, 26
Fuentes Quintana, Enrique, 82, 87–
88, 104, 105–106
Fueros, 26, 32, 117, 129
Fuerza Nueva, 118

Galicia, 54, 99, 121

Garrigues Walker, Joaquín, 62, 72, 82

Generalitat, 27–28, 85, 90

General Police Corps, 7, 93

General Workers' Union (UGT), 95–96, 111

generational change, 137

Gil Robles, José María, 66

Goiri, Sabino de Arana y. (*See*, Arana y Goiri, Sabino de)

González, Adolfo Suárez. (*See*, Suárez González, Adolfo)

González, Felipe, 49, 64, 79, 96, 115

GRAPO, 60, 91

Greece, 4

Guerra, Alfonso, 64, 115

Gutiérrez Mellado, Lt. General Manuel, 50, 82, 109, 139

Herrero Tejedor, Fernando, 44, 45

Historical Spanish Socialist Workers' Party (PSOE[h]), 63–64

Ibáñez Freire, Lt. General Antonio, 58

Ibarruri, Dolores, 49

ideology, 14, 63, 135, 136

immigration, 22, 30

imports, 102

inflation, 4, 46, 87, 92, 102, 110–111

Informaciones, 70

Iniesta Cano, General Carlos, 50

Interior, Ministry of, 89, 93

internal trade, 34–35

investment, 103

Irribarne, Manuel Fraga. (*See*, Fraga Irribarne, Manuel)

Isabel, Queen of Castile, 25

Italy, 4

Japan, 4

Jiménez, Joaquín Ruiz. (*See*, Ruiz Jiménez, Joaquín)

Juan Carlos, King: accession to throne of, 36; chooses Suárez as president of government, 44; confirms Arias Navarro as president of government, 37; on Constitution, 113; dismisses Arias, 43; first speech of. 36–37; names Fernández Miranda, 37–38; rejects call for constituent assembly, 47; relations of with army, 36, 50–51, 58; role of discussed, 137–139; mentioned *passim*

Judicial System, constitutional provisions on, 128

labor, 11–12, 93, 95–97

labor unions. (*See*, unions)

language, and regional nationalism, 34

Larroque, Enrique, 62

legalization, of political parties, 41–42, 56, 57–58

legislature, constitutional provisions on, 126–127

legitimacy, of Franco regime, 13, 14, 135

Lemóniz, 99

Letamendía, Francisco, 118

liberalism, 12, 26–27, 32, 35

Liberal Party, 62, 72

Liesa, Captain Francisco, 107

Linz, Juan, 18

Lister, General Enrique, 19

local politics, 94–95

local rights, 25–26, 32–33

López Raimundo, Gregorio, 69

López Rodó, Laureano, 1, 15, 68–69, 74

Luque, Alberto Monreal. (*See*, Monreal Luque, Alberto)

Lladó y Fernández-Urrutia, José, 82

Lliga regionalista, 27, 28

Maoists, 19

Marchais, Georges, 58

market economy, 132

Marxism, 10, 11, 67, 77

Marxist-Leninist Communist Party,

58–59

Matorell, Fernando Abril. (*See*, Abril Matorell, Fernando)

Mellado, General Manuel Gutiérrez. (*See*, Gutiérrez Mellado, General Manuel)

Miranda, Fernando Alvarez de. (*See*, Alvarez de Miranda, Fernando)

Miranda, Torcuato Fernández. (*See*, Fernández Miranda, Torcuato)

Mitterand, François, 64

monarchy, 25–26, 27, 44, 125–126

Moncloa Pact, 91–94, 96, 102–103, 139

Mondragón, 108–109

monetary policy, 46–47

money supply, 92

Monreal Luque, Alberto, 62

Motrico, Count of. (*See*, Areilza, José María de)

Múgica, Enrique, 115

municipal elections, 94–95

Napoleonic wars, 26

nationalism (regional). (*See*, autonomy, Basque Country, Canary Islands, Catalonia, Galicia, local rights, regionalism)

national movement, 9, 17, 135

national socialism, 14

national unity, government of, 79, 88–89

Navarre: and Basque Country, 91, 97–98, 99; history of, 28, 32, 33; results of constitutional referendum in, 124; University of, 131

Navarro, Carlos Arias. (*See*, Arias Navarro, Carlos)

Nenni, Pietro, 64

nuclear power plants, 98–99

Olarra, Luis, 89

Oliart Saussol, Alberto, 82

"Operation Galaxia," 109

opinion. (*See*, public opinion)

opposition: calls for constituent assembly, 47, 49; criticizes naming

of Suárez, 45; and December 1976 referendum, 51, 53; during Arias's government, 17, 40; during Franco regime, 17, 18; influence of on electoral law, 55–56; and Moncloa Pact, 91–94; negotiates with Suárez, 49–50, 54–55; refuses to accept legal status under June 1976 legislation, 56; support of for democratic institutions, 136–137

Opus Dei, 15

order. (*See*, public order)

Ordóñez, Francisco Fernández. (*See*, Fernández Ordóñez, Francisco)

Organization of African Unity, 101

Oriol y Urquijo, Antonio María de, 60

Osorio, Alfonso, 45

"Pact for Liberty," 19

Palme, Olof, 64

Pamplona, 106

pardon. (*See*, amnesty)

parliamentary responsibility, 81

participation, in politics, 16–17, 72, 74

parties, legalization of, 41, 48, 56–57, 57–58, 59

Peces-Barba, Gregorio, 64, 114

Peru, 6

Philip II, King, 25

Philip V, King, 26, 32

Pita da Veiga, Admiral Gabriel, 58

Platajunta. (*See*, *Democratic Coordination*)

police: charges of illegal wire-tapping by, 107; government's difficulty in controlling, 61; intensify patrolling in Basque Country, 108; reform of, 93; stage demonstrations, 107. (*See also*, armed police, civil guard, and General Police Corps)

political associations, 17

political prisoners, 13

Popular Alliance (AP), 62, 65–66, 68, 70, 74, 118

Popular Democratic Party, 62

Popular Movement for the Self-Determination and Independence of the Canarian Archipelago (MPAIAC), 100
Popular Party (PP), 62, 72
Popular Socialist Party (PSP), 64
popular sovereignty, 16
Portugal, 1, 4, 6, 17, 137
president of government, constitutional provisions on, 118, 125–126, 127–128
press, 9–10, 18, 70, 84
price controls, 46
Primo de Rivera, José Antonio, 14, 27, 136
prisons, 83
private property, 132
Professional Police Association, 107
proportional representation, 55–56
Plataforma de convergencia democrática, 39
public opinion, 16–17, 42, 47, 84
public order, 39, 60–62, 83–84, 89, 106, 107. (*See also*, demonstrations and strikes)
Pujol, Jordi, 69, 77

Quilis, Lt. General Emilio Villaescusa. (*See*, Villaescusa Quilis, Lt. General Emilio)
Quintana, Enrique Fuentes. (*See*, Fuentes Quintana, Enrique)

radio, 55, 93
railroads, 38–39
Raimundo, Gregorio López. (*See*, López Raimundo, Gregorio)
Ramos, Brigadier General Juan Sánchez. (*See*, Sánchez Ramos, Brigadier General Juan)
referendum: Arias schedules for October 1976, 40; on Constitution, 118–125; on Suárez's reforms, 51, 53
regional languages, 92, 129. (*See also*, Basque language and Catalan language)

regionalism: in Canary Islands, 21; in Catalonia and the Basque Country before 1975, 22–35; Church support of, 8; and December 1976 referendum, 51; in Galicia, 21; history of in Spain, 25–28, 32–34; and language, 34; as a political issue, 21, 28, 140–141; and poverty, 34; and taxes, 35; and trade among regions, 35. (*See also*, autonomy, Basque Country, Canary Islands, Catalonia, Galicia)
religion, freedom of, 130–132
Renaixença, 27
Rentería, 59, 106
republic. (*See*, Second Republic)
Reventós, Joan, 69, 77, 84, 115
right: appointment of Fernández Miranda designed to tranquilize, 37; attitude of toward Communists, 19–20, 48–49; denounces imitation of Europe, 17; opposition of to Suárez's reforms, 51; organizes demonstration for third anniversary of Franco's death, 109–110
right to work, 130
rights, constitutional provisions on, 130–132
Rivera, José Antonio Primo de. (*See*, Primo de Rivera, José Antonio)
Robles, José María Gil. (*See*, Gil Robles, José María)
Roca, Miguel, 115
Rodríguez de Sahagún, Agustín, 104
Rodríguez de Valcárcel, Alejandro, 37
Rubial, Ramón, 98
Ruiz Jiménez, Joaquín, 66
Ruptura democrática, 40

Sáenz de Inestrillas, Captain Ricardo, 109
Sahagún, Agustín Rodríguez de. (*See*, Rodríguez de Sahagún, Agustín)
Sánchez Ramos, Brigadier General

Juan, 106
Santiago, General Fernando de, 50
Saussol, Alberto Oliart. (*See*, Oliart Saussol, Alberto)
Second Carlist War, 32
Second Republic, 27–28
Second Vatican Council, 8
senate, 72, 117–118, 127, 133
Serer, Rafael Calvo. (*See*, Calvo Serer, Rafael)
S.E.U., 14
Silva Muñóz, Federico, 118
Social Democratic Grouping, 62
Social Democrats, 54, 67, 72
El Socialista, 70
socialists. (*See*, Federation of Socialist Parties, Historical Spanish Socialist Workers' Party, Popular Socialist Party, Socialists of Catalonia, Socialist Unity Coalition, and Spanish Socialist Workers' Party)
Socialists of Catalonia (SC), 69, 70, 77
Solé Tura, Jordi, 69, 115
Sotelo, Leopoldo Calvo. (*See*, Calvo Sotelo, Leopoldo)
Spanish Communist Party (PCE). (*See*, Communist Party)
Spanish Confederation of Business Organizations (CEOE), 97, 104
Spanish Democratic Union (UDE), 45, 62
Spanish Military Union, 7
Spanish National Union (UNE), 17
Spanish Social Democratic Party, 64
Spanish Socialist Workers' Party (PSOE): accepts Monarchy, 126; and Basque autonomy, 67; calls for resignation of Minister of Interior, 89; in Catalonia, 69; and constitutional provisions on education, 131; and constitutional provisions for election of Congress of Deputies, 126–127; and December 1976 referendum, 51; and election of President of Basque Council, 98; in elections, 64, 68, 70, 72, 74, 79–80; influence of on Moncloa Pact, 93; pacts of with UCD on Constitution, 115; refuses to join *Junta democrática*, 20; situation of at Franco's death, 18–19; 27th Congress of, 64; unwilling to join government of National Unity, 89; withdraws member from constitutional sub-committee, 105, 114
Spanish Unity Coalition, 64
State Party, 14
"Statute of Autonomy," 27
strikes, 11, 12, 16. (*See also*, demonstrations)
students, 10–11
Suárez González, Adolfo: acceptance speech of, 47; admits need for constituent assembly, 50; advocates legalization of parties, 41; and amnesty, 48, 59; announces intention of running for office, 63; and army, 50–51; attitude of toward Communist Party, 49, 58; background of, 17, 44–45; contribution of to democratization evaluated, 137–139; and December 1976 referendum, 51, 53; economic policy of, 46–47, 88, 104; faces crisis in Fall 1977, 88–90; first government of, 45–46; initial contacts of with opposition, 49; meets with Tarradellas, 84–85; and Moncloa Pact, 95– 94; and municipal elections, 94–95; named president of government, 44; and provisions of electoral law, 55–56; reaction to appointment of, 45; reaction of to January 1977 wave of violence, 60–61; reaction of to police protest, 107; and reestablishment of *Generalitat*, 90; reform proposals of, 49–51; rejects coalition government, 77, 79; relations of with the Democratic Center, 62–65; restructures government, 81–82,

83, 104, 105; strives to reconcile nation, 47; and union elections, 95–96; and the Union of the Spanish People, 45; victory of his candidates in elections, 72; visits Canary Islands, 100; mentioned *passim*, 44–124, 135–140
subway, 39
Supreme Court, 41–42, 58
syndicates, 11, 14

Tarradellas, Josep, 84–85, 90
taxes, 35, 46, 88, 92, 129
technocrats, 15
Tejero Molino, Lt. Colonel Antonio, 109
television, 55, 56, 71, 93
terrorism, 39, 91, 108–109. (*See also*, public order)
torture, 93
trade deficit, 46
Trias Fargas, Ramón, 69
Tura, Jordi Solé. (*See*, Solé Tura, Jordi)
Turkey, 4

unemployment, 4, 87–88, 92, 103, 111
Unified Socialist Party of Catalonia (PSUC), 69, 77
Union of the Spanish People (UDPE), 17, 45
unions: and businessmen, 13, 102–103; criticize Fuentes Quintana's emergency measures, 87–88; during Franco regime, 11–13; elections of officials of, 95–96; legislation on, 42, 54, 95–97; Suárez meets with leaders of, 88. (*See also*, General Workers'

Union, syndicates, and Workers' Commissions)
universal manhood suffrage, 47
universities, 10–11, 27
urbanization, 1
Urquijo, Antonio María de Oriol y. (*See*, Oriol y Urquijo, Antonio María de)

Valcárcel, Alejandro Rodríguez de. (*See*, Rodríguez de Valcárcel, Alejandro)
Valencia, 99
La Vanguardia, 70
Vatican, 8
Vega, Camilo Alonso. (*See*, Alonso Vega, Camilo)
Veiga, Admiral Gabriel Pita da. (*See*, Pita da Veiga, Admiral Gabriel)
Vicens Vives, Jaime, 35
Villaescusa Quilis, Lt. General Emilio, 60
Villar Mir, Juan Miguel, 42
violence. (*See*, public order and terrorism)
Vitoria, 39
Vives, Jaime Vicens. (*See*, Vicens Vives, Jaime)

wages, 38, 92, 102
Walker, Joaquín Garrigues. (*See* Garrigues Walker, Joaquín)
wire tapping, 107
Workers' Commissions, 11–12, 95–96, 103, 111, 139
Workers Revolutionary Organization (ORT), 58, 118

Ya, 70
Ybarra, Javier de, 86

ABOUT THE AUTHOR

JOHN F. COVERDALE is Associate Professor of History at North-western University, Evanston, Illinois. Until 1976, he was Assistant Professor of History at Princeton University, Princeton, New Jersey.

Professor Coverdale has published articles and reviews in the *Journal of Contemporary History, American Political Science Review,* and various Italian and Spanish publications. His *Italian Intervention in the Spanish Civil War* (Princeton, 1975), won the Howard R. Marraro Prize for the best book on Italian history. An Italian edition appeared in 1977 and a Spanish edition is in press.

Professor Coverdale holds a Ph.D. from the University of Wisconsin.